THE 21 INDISPENSABLE

QUALITIES OF
A LEADER

THE 21 INDISPENSABLE
QUALITIES OF
A LEADER

BECOMING *the* PERSON
OTHERS WILL WANT *to* FOLLOW

JOHN C.
MAXWELL

THOMAS NELSON
Since 1798

NASHVILLE   DALLAS   MEXICO CITY   RIO DE JANEIRO   BEIJING

Published in Nashville, Tennessee, by Thomas Nelson. Thomas Nelson is a registered trademark of Thomas Nelson, Inc.

Thomas Nelson, Inc., titles may be purchased in bulk for educational, business, fund-raising, or sales promotional use. For information, please e-mail SpecialMarkets@ThomasNelson.com.

Published in association with Yates & Yates, www.yates2.com

ISBN 978-0-7852-7440-7(hardcover)
ISBN 978-0-7852-8904-3 (repak)
ISBN 978-0-7852-6796-6 (IE)

Printed in the United States of America.

09 10 11 12 13 QW 13 12 11 10 9

CONTENTS

ACKNOWLEDGMENTS

I want to thank all of the people at Thomas Nelson who always work so hard and do such a fine job on my books.

I'd like to thank INJOY Group staff members—Linda Eggers, my administrative assistant; Brent Cole, my research assistant; and Stephanie Wetzel, my proofreader—all of whom make me better than I am.

And I must thank Charlie Wetzel, my writer, who multiplies my time and influence through his work.

INTRODUCTION

What makes people want to follow a leader? Why do people reluctantly comply with one leader while passionately following another to the ends of the earth? What separates leadership theorists from successful leaders who lead effectively in the real world? The answer lies in the character qualities of the individual person.

My friend, do you know whether you have what it takes to become a great leader, the kind who attracts people and makes things happen? I mean, if you took the time to really look at yourself deep down, would you find the qualities needed to live out your boldest dreams, the ones so big that you've never shared them with anybody? That's a question each of us must have the courage to honestly ask—and answer—if we want to achieve our real potential.

I've written this book to help you recognize, develop, and refine the personal characteristics needed to be a truly effective leader, the kind people *want* to follow. If you've already read

The 21 Irrefutable Laws of Leadership, then you understand that becoming a leader takes time. The Law of Process says that leadership develops daily, not in a day. Part of a leader's development comes from learning the laws of leadership, for those are the tools that teach how leadership works. But *understanding* leadership and actually *doing* it are two different activities.

Recently I talked to a friend named Bill Freeman. He is the president of Watkins Associated Industries, Inc., the largest privately owned trucking company in America. Bill is an excellent executive, and like all good leaders, he is continually looking for ways to learn and grow.

"I'm about halfway through your book," he told me, meaning *The 21 Irrefutable Laws of Leadership.* "It's making quite an impact on me." Then he said something that made quite an impact on *me.* "Let me tell you how I'm going through it," he said. "Each morning I read a chapter of the book. And all through the day, I think about that law. As I work, I look at myself and ask, How am I doing with this leadership law? I watch the people in the office, looking to see whether they practice it. I measure our whole company against it, observing, assessing, reflecting. Every morning it's a different law. It's an eye-opener."

Bill really got my juices flowing. In fact, his comments prompted me to write this book. He is approaching his own leadership development from the inside out, as he should. Leaders are effective because of who they are on the inside—in the qualities that make them up as people. And to go to the highest level of leadership, people have to develop these traits from the inside out.

After talking to Bill, I took some time to reflect on the characteristics of the best leaders I know, the ones who people really want to follow. I looked for common themes. I talked to other leaders and heard their impressions. And I examined leaders who have impacted history. I settled on a list of 21 qualities possessed by all great leaders. These traits are described and illustrated in this book, meant to be a complementary companion to *The 21 Irrefutable Laws of Leadership*.

As you dive into the book, you may find that you are able to easily breeze through several chapters at a time. You may even be able to knock out the whole book in one sitting. *Don't do it. The 21 Indispensable Qualities of a Leader* is designed to be absorbed the same way Bill Freeman approaches a book: strategically and methodically.

I want to encourage you to live with this book for a while. Read a chapter, and then give it some time. Use it to reflect, review, and renew. If the quality you're studying is a weak area in your life, spend some time addressing it before you move on to the next chapter. You may even want to repeat this process several times over the course of a year, cementing each trait into your character.

Everything rises and falls on leadership. And leadership truly develops from the inside out. If you can become the leader you *ought* to be on the *inside,* you will be able to become the leader you *want* to be on the *outside*. People will want to follow you. And when that happens, you'll be able to tackle anything in this world.

CHARACTER:

BE A PIECE OF THE ROCK

Leadership is the capacity and will
to rally men and women to a common purpose
and the character which inspires confidence.

—Bernard Montgomery,
British Field Marshal

Never "for the sake of peace and quiet"
deny your own experience or convictions.

—Dag Hammarskjöld,
Statesman and Nobel Peace Prize Winner

PUTTING IT ALL ON THE LINE

If you've traveled through smaller airports or have much experience flying in corporate aircraft, you've probably seen or flown in a Lear Jet. I've had the opportunity to fly in one a couple of times, and it's quite an experience. They're small—capable of carrying only five or six passengers—and very fast. It's like climbing into a narrow tube with jet engines strapped to it.

I have to admit, the whole experience of riding in a Lear Jet is pretty exhilarating. But by far the most amazing thing to me about it is the time it saves. I've traveled literally millions of miles on airlines, and I'm accustomed to long drives to airports, car rental returns, shuttles, terminal congestion, and seemingly endless delays. It can be a nightmare. Flying on a Lear Jet can easily cut travel time in half.

The father of this amazing airplane was a man named Bill Lear. An inventor, aviator, and business leader, Lear held more than 150 patents, including those of the automatic pilot, car radio, and eight-track tapes (you can't win them all). Lear was a pioneer in his thinking, and in the 1950s, he could see the potential for the manufacture of small corporate jets. It took him several years to make his dream a reality, but in 1963, the first Lear Jet made its maiden voyage, and in 1964 he delivered his first production jet to a client.

Lear's success was immediate, and he quickly sold many aircraft. But not long after he got his start, Lear learned that two aircraft he'd built had crashed under mysterious circumstances. He was devastated. At that time, fifty-five Lear Jets were privately owned, and

Lear immediately sent word to all of the owners to ground their planes until he and his team could determine what had caused the crashes. The thought that more lives might be lost was far more important to him than any adverse publicity that action might generate in the media.

As he researched the ill-fated flights, Lear discovered a potential cause, but he couldn't verify the technical problem on the ground. There was only one sure way to find out whether he had diagnosed the problem correctly. He would have to try to recreate it personally—in the air.

It was a dangerous process, but that's what he did. As he flew the jet, he nearly lost control and almost met the same fate as the other two pilots. But he did manage to make it through the tests, and he was able to verify the defect. Lear developed a new part to correct the problem and fitted all fifty-five planes with it, eliminating the danger.

Grounding the planes cost Lear a lot of money. And it planted seeds of doubt in the minds of potential customers. As a result, he needed two years to rebuild the business. But Lear never regretted his decision. He was willing to risk his success, his fortune, and even his life to solve the mystery of those crashes—but not his integrity. And that takes character.

FLESHING IT OUT

How a leader deals with the circumstances of life tells you many things about his character. Crisis doesn't necessarily make character, but it certainly does reveal it. Adversity is a crossroads that makes a person choose one of two paths: character or compromise. Every time he chooses character, he becomes stronger, even if that choice brings negative consequences. As Nobel prize–winning author Alexander Solzhenitsyn noted, "The meaning of earthly existing lies, not as we have grown used to thinking, in prospering, but in the development of the soul." The development of character is at the heart of our development not just as leaders, but as human beings.

What must every person know about character?

1. *Character Is More than Talk*
Anyone can *say* that he has integrity, but action is the real indicator of character. Your character determines who you are. Who you are determines what you see. What you see determines what you do. That's why you can never separate a leader's character from his actions. If a leader's actions and intentions are continually working against each other, then look to his character to find out why.

2. *Talent Is a Gift, but Character Is a Choice*
We have no control over a lot of things in life. We don't get to choose our parents. We don't select the location or circumstances of our birth and upbringing. We don't get to pick our talents or IQ. But we do choose our character. In fact, we create it every time we make choices—to cop out or dig out of a hard situation, to bend the truth or stand under the weight of it, to take

4

the easy money or pay the price. As you live your life and make choices today, you are continuing to create your character.

3. Character Brings Lasting Success with People

True leadership always involves other people. (As the leadership proverb says, if you think you're leading and no one is following you, then you're only taking a walk.) Followers do not trust leaders whose character they know to be flawed, and they will not continue following them.

4. Leaders Cannot Rise Above the Limitations of Their Character

Have you ever seen highly talented people suddenly fall apart when they achieved a certain level of success? The key to that phenomenon is character. Steven Berglas, a psychologist at Harvard Medical School and author of *The Success Syndrome,* says that people who achieve great heights but lack the bedrock character to sustain them through the stress are headed for disaster. He believes they are destined for one or more of the four A's: *arrogance,* painful feelings of *aloneness,* destructive *adventure-seeking,* or *adultery.* Each is a terrible price to pay for weak character.

REFLECTING ON IT

If you've found yourself being sucked in by one of the four A's that Berglas identifies, call a time-out. Do what you must to step away from some of the stress of your success, and seek professional help. Don't think that the valley you're in will pass with time, more money, or increased prestige. Unaddressed cracks in character only get deeper and more destructive with time.

If you're not struggling in any of these four areas, you should still examine the condition of your character. Ask yourself whether your words and actions match—all the time. When you say you'll finish an assignment, do you always follow through? If you tell your children that you'll make it to their recital or ball game, are you there for it? Can people trust your handshake as they would a legal contract?

As you lead others at home, at work, and in the community, recognize that your character is your most important asset. G. Alan Bernard, president of Mid Park, Inc., stated, "The respect that leadership must have requires that one's ethics be without question. A leader not only stays above the line between right and wrong, he stays well clear of the 'gray areas.'"

Bringing It Home

To improve your character, do the following:

- *Search for the cracks.* Spend some time looking at the major areas of your life (work, marriage, family, service, etc.), and identify anywhere you might have cut corners, compromised, or let people down. Write down every instance you can recall from the past two months.

- *Look for patterns.* Examine the responses that you just wrote down. Is there a particular area where you have a weakness, or do you have a type of problem that keeps surfacing? Detectable patterns will help you diagnose character issues.

- *Face the music.* The beginning of character repair comes when you face your flaws, apologize, and deal with the consequences of your actions. Create a list of people to whom you need to apologize for your actions, then follow through with sincere apologies.

- *Rebuild.* It's one thing to face up to your past actions. It's another to build a new future. Now that you've identified any areas of weakness, create a plan that will prevent you from making the same mistakes again.

DAILY TAKE-AWAY

A man took his young daughter to a carnival, and she immediately ran over to a booth and asked for cotton candy. As the attendant handed her a huge ball of it, the father asked, "Sweetheart, are you sure you can eat all that?"

"Don't worry, Dad," she answered, "I'm a lot bigger on the inside than on the outside."

That's what real character is—being bigger on the inside.

CHARISMA:
THE FIRST IMPRESSION CAN
SEAL THE DEAL

How can you have charisma? Be more concerned
about making others feel good about themselves than
you are making them feel good about you.

—Dan Reiland,
Executive Pastor at 12Stone Church in Lawrenceville, Georgia

I have yet to find the man,
however exalted his station, who did not
do better work and put forth greater effort under a
spirit of approval than under a spirit of criticism.

—Charles Schwab, Industrialist

T H E C L E V E R E S T I N E N G L A N D

During the second half of the nineteenth century, two strong men vied for leadership of Great Britain's government: William Gladstone and Benjamin Disraeli. The two politicians were intense rivals. You can detect how they felt about each other based on a comment once made by Disraeli: "The difference between a misfortune and a calamity? If Gladstone fell into the Thames [River], it would be a misfortune. But if someone dragged him out again, it would be a calamity."

Many people believe that Gladstone, leader of the Liberal Party for three decades, personified the best qualities of Victorian England. A career public servant, he was a great orator, a master of finance, and a staunchly moral man. He was made prime minister of the United Kingdom four different times, the only person in the nation's history to achieve that honor. Under his leadership, Great Britain established a national education system, instituted parliamentary reform, and saw the vote given to a significant number of people in the working classes.

Benjamin Disraeli, who served twice as prime minister, had a different kind of background. In his thirties, he entered politics and built a reputation as a diplomat and social reformer. But his greatest accomplishment was masterminding Great Britain's purchase of shares in the Suez Canal.

Though both men accomplished much for Britain, what really separated them as leaders was their approach to people. The difference can be best illustrated by a story told by a young woman who dined with the two rival statesmen on consecutive nights. When asked her impression of them, she said, "When I left the dining room after sitting next to Mr. Gladstone, I thought he was the cleverest *man* in England. But after sitting next to Mr. Disraeli, I thought I was the cleverest *woman* in England." Disraeli possessed a quality that drew people to him and made them want to follow him. He had charisma.

FLESHING IT OUT

Most people think of charisma as something mystical, almost undefinable. They think it's a quality that comes at birth or not at all. But that's not true. Charisma, plainly stated, is the ability to draw people to you. And like other character traits, it can be developed.

To make yourself the kind of person who attracts others, you need to personify these pointers:

1. Love Life

People enjoy leaders who enjoy life. Think of the people you want to spend time with. How would you describe them? Grumpy? Bitter? Depressed? Of course not. They're celebrators, not complainers. They're passionate about life. If you want to attract people, you need to be like the people you enjoy being with. Eighteenth-century evangelist John Wesley recognized that, saying, "when you set yourself on fire, people love to come and see you burn."

2. Put a "10" on Every Person's Head

One of the best things you can do for people—which also attracts them to you—is to expect the best of them. I call it putting a "10" on everyone's head. It helps others think more highly of themselves, and at the same time, it also helps you. According to Jacques Wiesel, "A survey of one hundred self-made millionaires showed only one common denominator. These highly successful men and women could only see the good in people."

Benjamin Disraeli understood and practiced this concept, and it was one of the secrets of his charisma. He once said, "The greatest good you can do for another is not just to share your riches but to reveal to him his own." If you appreciate others, encourage them, and help them reach their potential, they will love you for it.

3. Give People Hope

French General Napoleon Bonaparte characterized leaders as "dealers in hope." Like all great leaders, he knew that hope is the greatest of all possessions. If you can be the person who bestows that gift on others, they will be attracted to you, and they will be forever grateful.

4. Share Yourself

People love leaders who share themselves and their life journeys. As you lead people, give of yourself. Share wisdom, resources, and even special occasions. That's one of my favorite things to do. For example, I recently went to an annual storytelling festival in Jonesborough, Tennessee. It was something I had wanted to do for years, and when I was finally able to work it into my schedule, my wife, Margaret, and I took two leaders from my staff and their wives. We had a wonderful time, and more important, I was able to add value to their lives by spending special time with them.

When it comes to charisma, the bottom line is otherminded-ness. Leaders who think about others and their concerns before thinking of themselves exhibit charisma.

REFLECTING ON IT

How would you rate yourself when it comes to charisma? Are other people naturally attracted to you? Are you well liked? If not, you may possess one of these roadblocks to charisma:

Pride. Nobody wants to follow a leader who thinks he is better than everyone else.

Insecurity. If you are uncomfortable with who you are, others will be too.

Moodiness. If people never know what to expect from you, they stop expecting anything.

Perfectionism. People respect the desire for excellence, but dread totally unrealistic expectations.

Cynicism. People don't want to be rained on by someone who sees a cloud around every silver lining.

If you can stay away from these qualities, you can cultivate charisma.

To improve your charisma, do the following:

- *Change your focus.* Observe your interaction with people during the next few days. As you talk to others, determine how much of your conversation is concentrated on yourself. Determine to tip the balance in favor of focusing on others.

- *Play the first impression game.* Try an experiment. The next time you meet someone for the first time, try your best to make a good impression. Learn the person's name. Focus on his interests. Be positive. And most important, treat him as a "10." If you can do this for a day, you can do it every day. And that will increase your charisma overnight.

- *Share yourself.* Make it your long-term goal to share your resources with others. Think about how you can add value to five people in your life this year. They can be family members, colleagues, employees, or friends. Provide resources to help them grow personally and professionally, and share your personal journey with them.

D A I L Y   T A K E - A W A Y

Perle Mesta, the greatest Washington hostess since Dolley Madison, was asked the secret of her success in getting so many rich and famous people to attend her parties.

"It's all in the greetings and good-byes," she replied. When a guest arrived, she met him, saying, "At last you're here!" and as each left, she said, "I'm sorry you have to leave so soon!" Her agenda was to focus on others, not herself. That's charisma.

Commitment:

It Separates Doers from Dreamers

People do not follow uncommitted leaders.
Commitment can be displayed in a full range of
matters to include the work hours you choose to maintain,
how you work to improve your abilities, or what you
do for your fellow workers at personal sacrifice.

—Stephen Gregg,
Chairman and CEO of Ethix Corp.

He who has done his best
for his own time has lived for all times.

—Johann von Schiller, Playwright

OLD BEFORE HIS TIME

A couple of years ago, my wife, Margaret, and I had the opportunity to vacation in Italy. Our two greatest priorities were food and art. To find the finest food, we talked to friends who had been there. To see the finest artwork, we enlisted the help of a fantastic guide who is a buyer for New York's Metropolitan Museum of Art. During that tour we saw many great pieces of artwork. But none struck me the way Michelangelo's *David* did. That's when I understood why it is called a masterpiece.

Michelangelo lived an incredible life. Possibly the greatest artist of Western civilization—and certainly the most influential—he was born to sculpt. He once said that when he drank his wet nurse's milk as a baby, along with it came a love for the stonecutter's tools. He sculpted his first mature masterpiece at age twenty-one. He completed his *Pietà* and *David* before age thirty.

In his early thirties, Michelangelo was summoned to Rome by Pope Julius II to sculpt a magnificent papal tomb, but was then asked to work on a painting project instead. At first Michelangelo wanted to refuse, having no desire to paint a dozen figures on the ceiling of a small chapel in the Vatican. Though as a boy he had been trained to paint, his passion was sculpture. But when the pope pressed him, he reluctantly accepted the assignment.

Scholars believe Michelangelo's rivals pushed for him to get the job, hoping he would refuse it and lose favor with the pope, or take it and discredit himself. But once Michelangelo accepted the assignment, he thoroughly committed himself to it, expanding the project from a simple depiction of the twelve apostles to include more than four hundred figures and nine scenes from the book of Genesis.

For four grueling years, the artist lay on his back painting the ceiling of the Sistine Chapel. And he paid a great price. The work permanently damaged his eyesight and wore him down. Michelangelo said, "After four tortured years, more than four hundred over-life-sized figures, I felt as old and as weary as Jeremiah. I was only thirty-seven, yet friends did not recognize the old man I had become."

The impact of Michelangelo's commitment was far-reaching. He pleased his benefactor, the pope, and received other commissions from the Vatican. But more important, he made a huge impact in the artistic community. His Sistine Chapel frescoes were so boldly painted, so original, so exquisitely executed that they caused many fellow artists, including the gifted painter Raphael, to alter their style. Art historians maintain that Michelangelo's masterpiece forever changed the course of painting in Europe. And it laid a foundation for his equally important impact on sculpture and architecture.

Undoubtedly Michelangelo's talent created the potential for greatness, but without commitment, his influence would have been minimal. That level of commitment could be seen in his attention to the fine details as well as the overarching vision. When asked why he was working so diligently on a dark corner of the Sistine Chapel that no one would ever see, Michelangelo's simple reply was, "God will see."

The world has never seen a great leader who lacked commitment. Ed McElroy of USAir spoke of its importance: "Commitment gives us new power. No matter what comes to us—sickness, poverty, or disaster—we never turn our eye from the goal."

What is commitment? To each person, it means something different:

To the boxer, it's getting off the mat one time more than you've been knocked down.

To the marathoner, it's running another ten miles when your strength is gone.

To the soldier, it's going over the hill, not knowing what's waiting on the other side.

To the missionary, it's saying good-bye to your own comfort to make life better for others.

To the leader, it's all that and more because everyone you lead is depending on you.

If you want to be an effective leader, you have to be committed. True commitment inspires and attracts people. It shows them that you have conviction. They will believe in you only if you believe in your cause. As the Law of Buy-In states, people buy into the leader, then the vision.

What is the true nature of commitment? Take a look at three observations.

1. Commitment Starts in the Heart

Some people want everything to be perfect before they're willing to commit themselves to anything. But commitment always precedes achievement. I am told that in the Kentucky Derby, the winning horse effectively runs out of oxygen after the first half mile, and he goes the rest of the way on heart. That's why all great athletes recognize its importance. NBA legend Michael Jordan explains that "heart is what separates the good from the great." If you want to make a difference in *other* people's lives as a leader, look into *your* heart to see if you're really committed.

2. Commitment Is Tested by Action

It's one thing to talk about commitment. It's another to do something about it. The only *real* measure of commitment is action. Arthur Gordon acknowledged, "Nothing is easier than saying words. Nothing is harder than living them day after day."

Someone told me about a newly elected judge who had won office in a special county election. During his acceptance speech, he said, "I wish to thank the 424 people who promised to vote for me. I wish to thank the 316 people who said that they did vote for me. I wish to thank the 47 people who came out last Thursday to vote, and I wish to thank the 26 folks who actually did vote for me." How are you doing when it comes to following through on your commitments?

3. Commitment Opens the Door to Achievement
As a leader, you will face plenty of obstacles and opposition—if you don't already. And there will be times when commitment is the only thing that carries you forward. David McNally commented, "Commitment is the enemy of resistance, for it is the serious promise to press on, to get up, no matter how many times you are knocked down." If you want to get anywhere worthwhile, you must be committed.

REFLECTING ON IT

When it comes to commitment, there are really only four types of people:

1. *Cop-outs.* People who have no goals and do not commit.

2. *Holdouts.* People who don't know if they can reach their goals, so they're afraid to commit.

3. *Dropouts.* People who start toward a goal but quit when the going gets tough.

4. *All-outs.* People who set goals, commit to them, and pay the price to reach them.

What kind of person are you? Have you been reaching your goals? Are you achieving all that you believe you can? Do people believe in you and follow you readily? If your answer to any of these questions is no, the problem may be your level of commitment.

To improve your commitment, do the following:

- *Measure it.* Sometimes we *think* we are committed to something, yet our actions indicate otherwise. Take out your calendar and your checkbook register. Spend a few hours tallying up how you spend your time and where you spend your money. Look at how much time you spend at work, in service, with family, in health and recreation activities, and so forth. Figure out how much money you spent on living expenses, entertainment, personal development, and giving. All these things are true measures of your commitment. You may be surprised by what you find.

- *Know what's worth dying for.* One of the questions every leader must ask himself is, What am I willing to die for? If it came down to it, what in life would you not be able to stop doing, no matter what the consequences were? Spend some time alone meditating on that thought. Write down what you discover. Then see if your actions match your ideals.

- *Use the Edison method.* If taking the first step toward commitment is a problem, try doing what Thomas Edison did. When he had a good idea for an invention, he would call a press conference to announce it. Then he'd go into his lab and invent it. Make your plans public, and you might be more committed to following through with them.

DAILY TAKE-AWAY

Former pro basketball player Bill Bradley attended a summer basketball camp at age fifteen conducted by "Easy" Ed Macauley. During that camp, Macauley made a statement that changed Bradley's life: "Just remember that if you're not working at your game to the utmost of your ability, there will be someone out there somewhere with equal ability. And one day you'll play each other, and he'll have the advantage." How do you measure up against that standard?

COMMUNICATION:

WITHOUT IT YOU TRAVEL ALONE

Developing excellent communication skills is
absolutely essential to effective leadership. The leader
must be able to share knowledge and ideas to transmit a
sense of urgency and enthusiasm to others. If a leader can't
get a message across clearly and motivate others to act
on it, then having a message doesn't even matter.

—*Gilbert Amelio,*
President and CEO of National Semiconductor Corp.

Educators take something simple
and make it complicated. Communicators take
something complicated and make it simple.

—*John C. Maxwell*

A GREAT COMMUNICATOR
IN ALL CIRCUMSTANCES

Many American presidents have made an impact on our country as great communicators. John F. Kennedy, Franklin D. Roosevelt, and Abraham Lincoln come to mind as outstanding examples. But only one president in our lifetime was called the Great Communicator, and that was Ronald Reagan.

Flashes of Reagan's talent for communication revealed themselves early in his career. He started out in radio. In his early twenties, Reagan quickly became one of the best-known announcers in the Midwest. He usually announced games live, but occasionally he would simulate the broadcast of a Chicago Cubs game using Western Union reports of each play. During one such game, the wire went dead while Augie Galan was at bat in a tough situation. Reagan deftly kept Galan fouling off pitch after imaginary pitch for *six minutes* until he could pick up the play-by-play again.

Throughout his career, Reagan displayed an uncommon ability to connect and communicate with people. Nowhere was that more evident than during his time leading up to and in the White House. While announcing his run for the presidency in 1980, he cast the vision for his campaign clearly and simply, saying, "At the heart of our message should be five simple familiar words. No big economic theories. No sermons on political philosophy. Just five short words: *family, work, neighborhood, freedom, peace.*"

During his campaign, Reagan successfully debated incumbent Jimmy Carter. The former California governor came across as a relaxed, likable, competent middle American. He won easily. Afterward when asked if he had been nervous debating the president, Reagan answered, "No, not at all. I've been on the same stage with John Wayne."

Whether he was speaking to a group, looking into a camera, or connecting with someone one-on-one, Reagan was able to communicate with maximum effectiveness. Even when he was shot and was being wheeled into the operating room, his goal was to put others at ease. His comment to the surgeons was, "Please assure me that you are all Republicans."

Reagan was a good executive because he possessed a clear vision, made decisions easily, and delegated very effectively. But he was a great leader because of his uncanny ability to communicate. When it came to leading the country, people knew who he was, where he stood, and what he wanted, and they couldn't wait to get on board with him. Communication made him the kind of leader that people wanted to follow.

Fleshing It Out

Even if you don't have your sights set on leading the country, as Ronald Reagan did, you still need to possess the ability to communicate. The success of your marriage, job, and personal relationships depends greatly on it. People will not follow you if they don't know what you want or where you are going.

You can be a more effective communicator if you follow four basic truths.

1. Simplify Your Message

Communication is not just *what* you say. It's also how you say it. Contrary to what some educators teach, the key to effective communication is simplicity. Forget about impressing people with big words or complex sentences. If you want to connect with people, keep it simple. Napoleon Bonaparte used to tell his secretaries, "Be clear, be clear, be clear."

A story about a junior executive gives a blueprint for effective communication. The young man was invited to speak to a large group for the first time, so he approached his mentor for advice about giving a good speech. The older man said, "Write an exciting opening that will grab everybody in your audience. Then you write a dramatic summary and closing that will make the people want to act. Then put them as close together as possible."

2. See the Person

Effective communicators focus on the people with whom they're communicating. They know it is impossible to effectively communicate to an audience without knowing something about them.

As you communicate with people—whether individuals or groups—ask yourself these questions: Who is my audience? What are their questions? What needs to be accomplished? And how much time do I have? If you want to become a better communicator, become audience oriented. People believe in great communicators because great communicators believe in people.

3. Show the Truth

Credibility precedes great communication. There are two ways to convey credibility to your audience. First, believe in what you say. Ordinary people become extraordinary communicators when they are fired up with conviction. Field Marshal Ferdinand Foch observed, "The most powerful weapon on earth is the human soul on fire." Second, live what you say. There is no greater credibility than conviction in action.

4. Seek a Response

As you communicate, never forget that the goal of all communication is action. If you dump a bunch of information on people, you're not communicating. Every time you speak to people, give them something to feel, something to remember, and something to do. If you're successful in doing that, your ability to lead others will go to a new level.

R E F L E C T I N G   O N   I T

Danto Manquez Jr., president of MVM, Inc., has spoken to the issue of a leader's ability to communicate: "A leader must get things done through others, therefore the leader must have the ability to inspire and motivate, guide and direct, and listen. It's only through communication that the leader is able to cause others to internalize his or her vision and implement it."

How do you rate your ability to communicate with others? Is communication a priority for you? Can you inspire and motivate people? Do you express your vision in such a way that your people are able to understand, internalize, and implement it? When you talk to people one-on-one, are you able to connect with them? How about with groups? If you know in your heart that your vision is great, yet people still do not buy into it, your problem may be an inability to communicate effectively.

BRINGING IT HOME

To improve your communication, do the following:

- *Be clear as a bell.* Examine a letter, memo, or other item you've recently written. Are your sentences short and direct, or do they meander? Will your readers be able to grasp the words you've chosen, or will they have to scramble for a dictionary? Have you used the fewest words possible? To a communicator, your best friends are simplicity and clarity. Write your next piece of communication keeping both in mind.

- *Refocus your attention.* During the coming week, pay attention to your focus when you communicate. Is it on you, your material, or your audience? If it's not on people, you need to change it. Think about their needs, questions, and desires. Meet people where they are, and you will be a better communicator.

- *Live your message.* Are there any discrepancies between what you communicate and what you do? Talk to a few trustworthy people and ask them whether you are living your message. Your spouse, a mentor, or a close friend may be able to see things that you are blind to. Receive their comments without defensiveness. Then purpose to make changes in your life to be more consistent.

D A I L Y   T A K E - A W A Y

On April 7, 1865, President Abraham Lincoln made a burdensome decision, and he needed to communicate it to his general in the field. On it rested all his hopes and the entire weight of his leadership as president. Using all his considerable skill as a communicator, he wrote the following message:

Lieut. Gen. Grant,
Gen. Sheridan says, "If the thing is pressed, I think that Lee will surrender." Let the thing be pressed.
A. Lincoln

The president didn't allow the importance of a piece of communication to complicate its simplicity. Neither should we.

COMPETENCE:

IF YOU BUILD IT, THEY WILL COME

Competence goes beyond words.

It's the leader's ability to say it, plan it, and do it

in such a way that others know that you know how—

and know that they want to follow you.

—John C. Maxwell

The society which scorns excellence in plumbing

because plumbing is a humble activity and tolerates

shoddiness in philosophy because it is an exalted activity

will have neither good plumbing nor good philosophy.

Neither its pipes nor its theories will hold water.

—John Gardner, Author

F A N F A R E   F O R   A   C O M M O N   M A N

Benjamin Franklin always thought of himself as an ordinary citizen. One of seventeen children, Franklin was the son of a tradesman, a candlemaker, who was far from wealthy. He experienced a typical childhood. He attended school for only two years, and at age twelve, he was apprenticed to his brother in the printing trade.

Franklin worked hard and lived a simple life, governing his actions according to a set of thirteen virtues, upon which he graded himself daily. At age twenty he started his own printing business. Had Franklin been content to work at his trade, his name would be little more than a footnote in Philadelphia's history. Yet he lived an extraordinary life. He was one of the fathers of American independence and a great leader of the emerging nation. He coauthored the Declaration of Independence, and he later helped write the Treaty of Paris and the Constitution of the United States. (He was the only man who signed all three.) And he was selected to perform a difficult and dangerous secret diplomatic mission to Paris during the war to secure military and financial support for the Revolution.

What gave a northern tradesman the opportunity to exert so much influence among the wealthy, predominately southern landholders who headed the war for independence? I believe it was Franklin's incredible competence.

Benjamin Franklin excelled at everything he touched for seven decades. When he started his own printing business in 1726, people believed Philadelphia could not support a third printer, but Franklin quickly established a reputation as the most skilled and industrious printer in town. But the Philadelphia tradesman wasn't content with only that accomplishment.

Franklin's mind was curious, and he continually sought ways to improve himself and others. He expanded into publishing, his work including the noted *Poor Richard's Almanack*. He did extensive experiments with electricity and coined many of the terms still associated with its use. He invented numerous items such as the potbellied stove, the catheter, and bifocals. And when he traveled frequently across the Atlantic Ocean, he took it upon himself to chart the Gulf Stream. His attitude toward life could be seen in an aphorism he wrote for his almanac: "Hide not your talents. They for use were made. What's a sundial in the shade?"

The evidences of Franklin's talents were many. He helped establish Philadelphia's first library. He started the nation's first fire department. He developed the concept of daylight saving time. And he held many posts serving the government.

For the most part, Franklin was recognized for his ability. But sometimes he had to let his competence speak for itself. During a time when he was working on improvements in agriculture, he discovered that plaster made grains and grasses grow better, but he had a difficult time convincing his neighbors about the discovery. His solution? When spring arrived, he went to a field close to a path, dug out some letters into the dirt with his hands, put plaster into the ruts, and then sowed seed over the whole area. As people passed that way in following weeks, they could see green letters growing brighter than the rest of the field. They said simply, "This has been plastered." People got the message.

We all admire people who display high competence, whether they are precision craftsmen, world-class athletes, or successful business leaders. But the truth is that you don't have to be Fabergé, Michael Jordan, or Bill Gates to excel in the area of competence. If you want to cultivate that quality, here's what you need to do.

1. Show Up Every Day

There's a saying, "All things come to him who waits." Unfortunately sometimes it's just the leftovers from the people who got there first. Responsible people show up when they're expected. But highly competent people take it a step farther. They don't show up in body only. They come ready to play every day—no matter how they feel, what kind of circumstances they face, or how difficult they expect the game to be.

2. Keep Improving

Like Benjamin Franklin, all highly competent people continually search for ways to keep learning, growing, and improving. They do that by asking *why*. After all, the person who knows *how* will always have a job, but the person who knows *why* will always be the boss.

3. *Follow Through with Excellence*

I've never met a person I considered competent who didn't follow through. I bet it's the same for you. Willa A. Foster remarked, "Quality is never an accident; it is always the result of high intention, sincere effort, intelligent direction and skillful execution; it represents the wise choice of many alternatives."

Performing at a high level of excellence is always a choice, an act of the will. As leaders, we expect our people to follow through when we hand them the ball. They expect that and a whole lot more from us as their leaders.

4. *Accomplish More than Expected*

Highly competent people always go the extra mile. For them, good enough is never good enough. In *Men in Mid-Life Crisis,* Jim Conway writes that some people feel "a weakening of the need to be a great man and an increasing feeling of 'let's just get through this the best way we can.' Never mind hitting home runs. Let's just get through the ball game without getting beaned." Leaders cannot afford to have that kind of attitude. They need to do the job, and then some, day in and day out.

5. *Inspire Others*

Highly competent leaders do more than perform at a high level. They inspire and motivate their people to do the same. While some people rely on relational skills alone to survive, effective leaders combine these skills with high competence to take their organizations to new levels of excellence and influence.

Where do you stand when it comes to getting the job done? Do you attack everything you do with fervor and perform at the highest level possible? Or is good enough sometimes good enough for you?

When you think about people who are competent, you're really considering only three types of people:

1. Those who can see what needs to happen.

2. Those who can make it happen.

3. Those who can make things happen when it really counts.

When it comes to your profession, where do you consistently perform? Are you a thinker, a doer, or a clutch player? The better you are, the greater potential for influence you will have with your people.

To improve your competence, do the following:

• *Get your head in the game.* If you've been mentally or emotionally detached from your work, it's time to reengage. First, rededicate yourself to your job. Determine to give it an appropriate amount of your undivided attention. Second, figure out why you have been detached. Do you need new challenges? Are you in conflict with your boss or coworkers? Are you in a dead-end job? Identify the source of the problem, and create a plan to resolve it.

- *Redefine the standard.* If you're not performing at a consistently high level, reexamine your standards. Are you shooting too low? Do you cut corners? If so, hit your mental reset button, and outline more demanding expectations for yourself.

- *Find three ways to improve.* Nobody keeps improving without being intentional about it. Do a little research to find three things you can do to improve your professional skills. Then dedicate the time and money to follow through on them.

DAILY TAKE-AWAY

I read an editorial in *Texas Business* not long ago that said, "We are truly the lost generation, huffing and puffing down the fast track to nowhere, always looking to the dollar sign for direction. That's the only standard we recognize. We have no built-in beliefs, no ethical boundaries."

You're only as good as your private standards. When was the last time you gave a task your absolute best even though nobody but you would know about it?

COURAGE:

ONE PERSON WITH COURAGE

IS A MAJORITY

Courage is rightly esteemed the
first of human qualities . . . because it is the
quality which guarantees all others.

—*Winston Churchill, British Prime Minister*

Courage is fear that has said its prayers.

—*Karl Barth, Swiss Theologian*

THE ACE OF ACES

What do these three men have in common: the auto racer who set the world speed record at Daytona in 1914, the pilot who recorded the highest number of victories in aerial combat against the Germans in World War I, and the secretary of war's special adviser who survived a plane crash and twenty-two days on a raft in the Pacific during World War II? They all lived through dangerous circumstances. They all displayed courage and steely nerves under duress. And they all happen to be the same person—Eddie Rickenbacker.

Meeting a challenge was never a big problem for Eddie Rickenbacker, whether it was physical, mental, or economic. When he was twelve, his father died, and he quit school to become the family's primary breadwinner. He sold newspapers, eggs, and goat's milk. He worked in a glass factory, brewery, shoe factory, and foundry. Then as a teenager, he started working as a race car mechanic, and at age twenty-two, he began racing. Two years later he set the world speed record.

When the United States entered World War I, Rickenbacker tried to enlist as an aviator, but he was overage and undereducated. So instead he entered as a chauffeur and then talked his superiors into sending him to flight training. Despite not fitting in with his college-educated fellow aviators, he excelled as a pilot. And by the time the war was over, he had logged 300 combat hours (the most of any American pilot), survived 134 aerial encounters with the enemy, claimed 26 kills, and earned the

Medal of Honor, eight Distinguished Service Crosses, and the French Legion of Honor. He was also promoted to captain and put in command of his squadron.

Rickenbacker's prowess in the air caused the press to dub him the "American Ace of Aces." When asked about his courage in combat, he admitted that he had been afraid. "Courage," he said, "is doing what you're afraid to do. There can be no courage unless you're scared."

That courage served the Ace of Aces well after World War I. In 1933, he became the vice president of Eastern Air Transport (later Eastern Airlines). Back then all airlines existed only because they were subsidized by the government. But Rickenbacker thought they should be self-sufficient. He decided to completely change the way the company did business. Within two years he made Eastern profitable, a first in aviation history. And when the president of the United States canceled all commercial carriers' air mail contracts, Rickenbacker took him on—and won. Rickenbacker led Eastern successfully for thirty years and retired at age seventy-three. When he died ten years later, his son, William, wrote, "If he had a motto, it must have been the phrase I've heard a thousand times: 'I'll fight like a wildcat!'"

FLESHING IT OUT

When you look at the life of someone like Eddie Rickenbacker, you cannot help seeing great courage. It's easy to see in war heroes, but it's also present in every great leader in business, government, and the church. Whenever you see significant progress in an organization, you know that the leader made courageous decisions. A leadership position doesn't give a person courage, but courage can give him a leadership position. That was true for Captain Eddie Rickenbacker.

Larry Osborne offers this observation: "The most striking thing about highly effective leaders is how little they have in common. What one swears by, another warns against. But one trait stands out: the willingness to risk."

As you approach the tough decisions that challenge you, recognize these truths about courage:

1. Courage Begins with an Inward Battle

Every test you face as a leader begins within you. The test of courage is no different. As psychotherapist Sheldon Kopp notes, "All the significant battles are waged within self." Courage isn't an absence of fear. It's doing what you are afraid to do. It's having the power to let go of the familiar and forge ahead into new territory. That was true for Rickenbacker, and it can be true for you.

2. Courage Is Making Things Right, Not Just Smoothing Them Over

Civil rights leader Martin Luther King Jr. declared, "The ultimate measure of a man is not where he stands in moments of comfort and convenience, but where he stands at times of challenge and controversy." Great leaders have good people skills, and they can get people to compromise and work together. But they also take a stand when needed.

Courage deals with principle, not perception. If you don't have the ability to see when to stand up and the conviction to do it, you'll never be an effective leader. Your dedication to potential must remain stronger than your desire to appease others.

3. Courage in a Leader Inspires Commitment from Followers

"Courage is contagious," asserts evangelist Billy Graham. "When a brave man takes a stand, the spines of others are stiffened." A show of courage by any person encourages others. But a show of courage by a leader inspires. It makes people want to follow him. My friend Jim Mellado explains, "Leadership is the expression of courage that compels people to do the right thing."

4. Your Life Expands in Proportion to Your Courage

Fear limits a leader. Roman historian Tacitus wrote, "The desire for safety stands against every great and noble enterprise." But courage has the opposite effect. It opens doors, and that's one of its most wonderful benefits. Perhaps that's why British theologian John Henry Newman said, "Fear not that your life will come to an end but that it will never have a beginning." Courage not only gives you a good beginning, but it also provides a better future.

What's ironic is that those who don't have the courage to take risks and those who do, experience the same amount of fear in life. The only difference is that those who don't take chances worry about trivial things. If you're going to have to overcome your fear and doubts anyway, you might as well make it count.

REFLECTING ON IT

Eleanor Roosevelt acknowledged, "You gain strength, courage, and confidence by every experience in which you really stop to look fear in the face. You are able to say to yourself, 'I lived through this horror. I can take the next thing that comes along.' You must do the thing you think you cannot do."

How do you tend to handle fear? Do you embrace it? Are stretching experiences a regular part of your daily life? Or have you retreated so far into your comfort zone that you don't ever even feel fear? How must you change to develop a spirit of courage in your life?

BRINGING IT HOME

To improve your courage, do the following:

- *Face the music.* Go out and do something stretching simply for the sake of growing in courage. Skydive. Speak in front of an audience (most people's greatest fear). Perform in a play. Go white-water rafting. Rock climb. It doesn't matter what you do as long as it causes you to face a genuine fear.

- *Talk to* that *person.* Most people are avoiding confrontation with someone in their lives—an employee, a relative, or a coworker. If that's true for you, talk to that person this week. Don't dump on him or abuse him. Speak the truth in love. (You won't be so afraid to do it if you've already sky-dived rafted, etc.)

- *Take a giant step.* Maybe you've been afraid to make a career move. If you've known in your heart that you should have changed jobs or started that new business, now is the time to face up to it. Take the time to really look at it. Talk to your spouse, your mentor, and a trusted friend or two. If it's the right thing to do, then *do it.*

DAILY TAKE-AWAY

A nineteenth-century circuit-riding preacher named Peter Cartwright was preparing to deliver a sermon one Sunday when he was warned that President Andrew Jackson was in atten-dance, and he was asked to keep his remarks inoffensive. During that message, he included these statements: "I have been told that Andrew Jackson is in this congregation. And I have been asked to guard my remarks. What I must say is that Andrew Jackson will go to hell if he doesn't repent of his sin."

After the sermon, Jackson strode up to Cartwright. "Sir," the president said, "if I had a regiment of men like you, I could whip the world."

A courageous act often brings unexpected positive results.

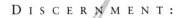

DISCERNMENT:

PUT AN END TO UNSOLVED MYSTERIES

Smart leaders believe only half of what they hear.
Discerning leaders know *which* half to believe.

—*John C. Maxwell*

The first rule of holes:
When you're in one, stop digging.

—*Molly Ivins, Columnist*

A L W A Y S   A T   T H E
H E A R T   O F   T H E   M A T T E R

Marya Sklodowska always wanted to get to the heart of things. As a child growing up in Poland, she loved school and learning. When her parents lost their teaching jobs and took in boarders to survive, she spent endless hours helping with the chores. But that didn't stop her from finishing first in her high school class—and her exams were in Russian!

Since higher education wasn't available to her, she became a governess and tutor. Somehow she managed to save enough money to send her older sister through medical school in Paris. Then she also moved to France to study at the Sorbonne. Two years later she finished first in her class in physics. Another year of study earned her a master's degree in mathematics.

It was then that she turned her attention full time to research, conducting experiments for a French industrial society. But her real passion was searching for the secret to uranium's rays.

While looking for a better laboratory, Marya met the man who would become her husband and research partner, Pierre. You've probably heard of Marya Sklodowska, but it's likely that you learned the name she preferred after she married Pierre Curie in 1895: she called herself Madame Marie Curie.

Madame Curie went on to do groundbreaking work in the field of radioactivity (a term she coined), and she opened the door to the study of nuclear physics and modern medical radiology. And when Pierre died in an accident in 1906, Marie Curie continued the work and made many additional breakthroughs.

"Life is not easy for any of us," she once said. "But what of that? We must have perseverance and above all confidence in ourselves. We must believe that we are gifted for something and that this thing must be attained." Her research brought her great recognition: fifteen gold medals, nineteen degrees, and two Nobel prizes (one in physics and one in chemistry).

Curie's tenacity was evident not only in her desire to know, but also in her practical application of her research. During World War I, she noted what was happening on the battlefields and recognized that the technology she had discovered could help save lives. She and her daughter Irene (who would later also win a Nobel prize) developed X-radiography and then led a movement to equip ambulances with X-ray equipment. And Curie trained 150 technicians to use it. Curie also helped found the Radium Institute at the University of Paris. Not only did she oversee the building of its laboratories, but she raised funds and materials in Europe and the United States to equip it.

Curie observed, "Nothing in life is to be feared. It is only to be understood." Her intelligence and discernment allowed her to understand and discover many things that have made a positive impact on our world. Unfortunately keen discernment did not extend to her health. Because she was on the cutting edge of research with radioactive materials, she did not protect herself from the effects of radiation. Her work slowly killed her. Rather suddenly, her health declined, and in 1934, she died of leukemia at age sixty-six.

F L E S H I N G   I T   O U T

Discernment can be described as the ability to find the root of the matter, and it relies on intuition as well as rational thought. Effective leaders need discernment, although even good leaders don't display it all the time. For example, read these comments made by leaders, which I like to think of as famous last words:

> "I tell you Wellington is a bad general, the English are bad soldiers; we will settle the matter by lunch time."
> —*Napoleon Bonaparte at breakfast with his generals preceding the Battle of Waterloo (1815)*

> "I think there is a world market for about five computers."
> —*Thomas J. Watson, chairman of IBM (1943)*

> "I don't need bodyguards."
> —*Jimmy Hoffa, one month before his disappearance (1975)*

Discernment is an indispensable quality for any leader who desires to maximize effectiveness. It helps to do several important things:

1. Discover the Root Issues

Leaders of large organizations must cope with tremendous chaos and complexity every day. They are never able to gather enough information to get a complete picture of just about anything. As a result, they have to rely on discernment. Researcher Henry

Mintzberg of McGill University stated, "Organizational effectiveness does not lie in that narrowminded concept called rationality. It lies in the blend of clearheaded logic and powerful intuition." Discernment enables a leader to see a partial picture, fill in the missing pieces intuitively, and find the real heart of a matter.

2. Enhance Your Problem Solving

If you can see the root issue of a problem, you can solve it. The closer a leader is to his area of gifting, the stronger his intuition and ability to see root causes. If you want to tap into your discernment potential, work in your areas of strength.

3. Evaluate Your Options for Maximum Impact

Management consultant Robert Heller has this advice: "Never ignore a gut feeling, but never believe that it's enough." Discernment isn't relying on intuition alone, nor is it relying only on intellect. Discernment enables you to use both your gut and your head to find the best option for your people and your organization.

4. Multiply Your Opportunities

People who lack discernment are seldom in the right place at the right time. Although great leaders often appear to be lucky to some observers, I believe leaders create their own "luck" as the result of discernment, that willingness to use their experience and follow their instincts.

R E F L E C T I N G   O N   I T

Are you a discerning leader? When faced with complex issues, can you readily identify the heart of the matter? Are you able to see root causes of difficult problems without having to get every bit of information? Do you trust your intuition and rely on it as much as you do your intellect and experience? If not, you need to cultivate it. Value nontraditional thinking. Embrace change, ambiguity, and uncertainty. Broaden your horizons experientially. Your intuition will only increase with use.

B R I N G I N G   I T   H O M E

To improve your discernment, do the following:

- *Analyze past successes.* Look at some problems you solved successfully in the past. What was the root issue in each problem? What enabled you to succeed? If you can capture the heart of the matter in a few words, you can probably learn to do it with future issues.

- *Learn how others think.* Which great leaders do you admire? Pick some whose profession or gifting is similar to yours, and read their biographies. By learning how other discerning leaders think, you can become more discerning.

- *Listen to your gut.* Try to recall times when your intuition "spoke" to you and was correct (you may or may not have listened to it at the time). What do those experiences have in common? Look for a pattern that may give you insight into your intuitive ability.

DAILY TAKE-AWAY

For a long time, the Swiss had a lock on watchmaking. They built the best watches money could buy, and by the 1940s, they produced 80 percent of all watches worldwide. In the late 1960s, when an inventor presented an idea for a new type of watch to the leaders of a Swiss watch company, they rejected it. In fact, every Swiss company he approached had the same negative reaction.

Believing his design had merit, the man took it to a company in Japan. The name of the organization was Seiko, the design of the watch was digital, and today, 80 percent of all watches use a digital design. One discernment-driven decision can change the entire course of your destiny.

If you chase two rabbits, both will escape.

—*Unknown*

What people say, what people do, and
what they say they do are entirely different things.

—*Margaret Mead, Anthropologist*

A DIFFERENT KIND
OF ONE-TRACK MIND

In 1998, the Atlanta Braves and the San Diego Padres played for major-league baseball's National League pennant, and I had the privilege of attending several of the games. Back when I lived in San Diego, I was a die-hard Padres fan, but when I moved to Atlanta in 1997, I changed my allegiance to the Braves. I rooted for them all season long—until they faced San Diego in the play-offs. Why did I change? I could not bring myself to root against Tony Gwynn.

Tony Gwynn is the greatest hitter in the last fifty years—the best since Ted Williams. He has won an incredible eight batting titles. (Only Ty Cobb has won more.) In his career, he has batted a tremendous .339. It's always a joy to watch Gwynn play. He is surely destined for the Hall of Fame in Cooperstown, New York.

If you saw Tony Gwynn on the street and didn't know who he was, you might not guess he was a professional ballplayer. At five feet eleven inches and 220 pounds, he doesn't look the part of the star athlete the way someone like Mark McGwire does. But make no mistake: Gwynn is a talented athlete, having been drafted out of college for baseball and basketball. And though he has tremendous talent, the real key to his success is focus.

Tony Gwynn loves hitting a baseball, and he *devotes* himself to it. Several times each season, he reads Ted Williams's *The Science of Hitting,* a book he first discovered and read while in college. He watches countless hours of videotape. At home he has a library of hitting tapes, continually fed by his five VCRs that record games via satellite dish. He even reviews tape on the road. When he travels for games, he takes two VCRs so that he can tape and edit every one of his at bats. And when he is not swinging the bat or watching tape, he is talking about hitting constantly—with teammates, at the All-Star Game, with great players such as Ted Williams.

Gwynn just can't get enough. Hitting is his joy. He has been known to arrive at social events with a batting glove sticking out of his pocket, having stopped to hit a few. And even when not practicing, watching tape, or talking to other hitters, he can be found playing Ping-Pong or doing activities to improve his eye-to-hand coordination. Even his decision to remain in San Diego his whole career has improved his game. "One of my strengths is knowing how much I can handle," Gwynn says. "There are few distractions in San Diego. There isn't a lot of media hoopla. That helps me be consistent."

Consistent is right. Gwynn has batted over .300 in every season as a professional except one—his first. Columnist George Will maintains that people who are great at what they do, such as Gwynn, have "cultivated a kind of concentration unknown to most people."

Fleshing It Out

What does it take to have the focus required to be a truly effective leader? The keys are priorities and concentration. A leader who knows his priorities but lacks concentration knows what to do but never gets it done. If he has concentration but no priorities, he has excellence without progress. But when he harnesses both, he has the potential to achieve great things.

I frequently meet people in leadership positions who seem to major in minor things. That just doesn't make sense. It would be the equivalent of Tony Gwynn spending all his time studying base stealing. Now, Gwynn *can* steal bases. He has stolen more than three hundred in his career, but it's not his strength. And dedicating all his time to that instead of hitting would be a waste of his time and talent.

So the important question is, How should you focus your time and energy? Use these guidelines to help you:

Focus 70 Percent on Strengths
Effective leaders who reach their potential spend more time focusing on what they do well than on what they do wrong. Leadership expert Peter Drucker notes, "The great mystery isn't that people do things badly but that they occasionally do a few things well. The only thing that is universal is incompetence. Strength is always specific! Nobody ever commented, for example, that the great violinist Jascha Heifetz probably couldn't play the trumpet very well." To be successful, focus on your strengths and develop them. That's where you should pour your time, energy, and resources.

Focus 25 Percent on New Things
Growth equals change. If you want to get better, you have to keep changing and improving. That means stepping out into new

areas. Gwynn modeled that several years ago after he had a conversation with Ted Williams. The old pro suggested that learning to hit inside pitches would make Gwynn a better player. Gwynn, who preferred outside balls, worked on it, and his average went up significantly. If you dedicate time to new things related to areas of strength, then you'll grow as a leader. Don't forget: in leadership, if you're through growing, you're through.

Focus 5 Percent on Areas of Weakness

Nobody can entirely avoid working in areas of weakness. The key is to minimize it as much as possible, and leaders can do it by delegating. For example, I delegate detail work to others. A team of people at The INJOY Group handles all the logistics of my conferences. That way when I'm there, I stick to the things I do best, such as the actual speaking.

R E F L E C T I N G   O N   I T

How would you rate yourself in the area of focus? Have you been majoring in minor things? Have you spent so much time shoring up your weaknesses that you've failed to build up your strengths? Do the people with the least potential monopolize your time? If so, you've probably lost focus.

To get back on track with your focus, do these things:

Work on yourself. You are your greatest asset or detriment.
Work at your priorities. You will have to fight for them.

Work in your strengths. You can reach your potential.

Work with your contemporaries. You can't be effective alone.

B R I N G I N G   I T   H O M E

To improve your focus, do the following:

- *Shift to strengths.* Make a list of three or four things you do well in your job. What percentage of your time do you spend doing them? What percentage of your resources is dedicated to these areas of strength? Devise a plan to make changes, allowing you to dedicate 70 percent of your time to your strengths. If you can't, it may be time to reassess your job or career.

- *Staff your weaknesses.* Identify three or four activities necessary for your job that you don't do well. Determine how you can delegate the jobs to others. Will it require hiring staff? Can you partner with a coworker to share responsibilities? Develop a plan.

- *Create an edge.* Now that you've looked at priorities, think about concentration. What would it take for you to go to the next level in your main area of strength? What new tools do you need? Rethink how you do things, and be willing to make sacrifices. Time and money spent to take you to the next level are the best investment you can make.

D A I L Y   T A K E - A W A Y

Experienced animal trainers take a stool with them when they step into a cage with a lion. Why a stool? It tames a lion better than anything—except maybe a tranquilizer gun. When the trainer holds the stool with the legs extended toward the lion's face, the animal tries to focus on all four legs at once. And that paralyzes him. Divided focus always works against you.

GENEROSITY:

YOUR CANDLE LOSES NOTHING

WHEN IT LIGHTS ANOTHER

No person was ever honored for what he received.
Honor has been the reward for what he gave.

—Calvin Coolidge, American President

Giving is the highest level of living.

—John C. Maxwell

IT STARTS IN THE HEART

When you think of generous people, who comes to mind? Do you picture millionaire philanthropists from the turn of the century such as Andrew Carnegie, J. P. Morgan, and Andrew Mellon? Do you think of contemporary givers such as Joan Kroc or Bill Gates? Those people have given away millions of dollars. But I want to acquaint you with another giver. She is someone you've probably never heard of, yet she typifies the deepest kind of giving, the kind that can come only from the heart.

Her name is Elisabeth Elliot. In the early 1950s, she accompanied a group of missionaries to Ecuador with the hope of reaching the Quichua Indians. Among that group was a young man named Jim, who had been courting her since 1947. While they worked together and gave their lives to serving the Ecuadoran Indians, they finally decided to give themselves to each other and were married.

They had been together about two years and had a ten-month-old daughter named Valerie when Jim and four other missionaries felt compelled to make contact with another small group of Indians living in the area called the Auca. The Indians had a fierce reputation. The earliest record of any contact with them was of their killing a priest in the 1600s. Since then, they had attacked every outsider who came their way. Even the other Ecuadoran Indians avoided them because of their brutality.

As Jim and the others prepared to make contact, Elisabeth knew that the five men would be putting themselves in danger, but she was resolute. The two of them had given their lives to this mission. For several weeks, a missionary pilot flew a small plane over an Aucan village and dropped supplies and other items as gifts. They even included pictures of themselves to prepare the tribespeople for their first contact.

A few weeks later, Jim and four others landed on a small stretch of beach on the Curaray River and set up camp. There they made contact with three Aucans—a man and two women—who seemed to be friendly and receptive. And in following days, they met with several others. They told their wives by radio that they seemed to be making significant progress in befriending the tribe.

But then a few days later, the men failed to check in with the base camp at an appointed time. Their wives waited in vain to hear from them. Minutes passed, then hours, and then a day. Elisabeth and the others feared the worst.

A search party went out to look for the men and radioed back bad news. They had spotted the body of a white man floating in the river. The searchers found the men, one by one. With each it was the same: he had been slashed with Aucan spears. All five of the men were dead.

Under those circumstances, many people in Elisabeth Elliot's shoes would have gone home. It's one thing to be willing to give up a comfortable life in the United States to help other people; it's quite another to give up your spouse. But Elliot had a truly generous heart. Despite her terrible loss, she still wanted to help the people of Ecuador. She stayed and served the Quichuans with whom she was living.

What happened after that is even more remarkable. Other missionaries continued trying to make contact with an Aucan village. And after a couple of years, they succeeded. Immediately Elisabeth Elliot rushed to the village. Was it to seek revenge? No, it was to work with the people there and serve them. Elliot lived and worked among the Aucan people for two years, and many of them gladly accepted the message of God's love she carried—including two of the seven men who had killed her husband.

FLESHING IT OUT

Nothing speaks to others more loudly or serves them better than generosity from a leader. True generosity isn't an occasional event. It comes from the heart and permeates every aspect of a leader's life, touching his time, money, talents, and possessions. Effective leaders, the kind that people want to follow, don't gather things just for themselves; they do it in order to give to others. Cultivate the quality of generosity in your life. Here's how:

1. Be Grateful for Whatever You Have
It's hard for a person to be generous when he is not satisfied with what he has. Generosity rises out of contentment, and that doesn't come with acquiring more. Millionaire John D. Rockefeller admitted, "I have made millions, but they have brought me no happiness." If you're not content with little, you won't be content with a lot. And if you're not generous with little, you won't suddenly change if you become wealthy.

2. Put People First

The measure of a leader is not the number of people who serve him, but the number of people he serves. Generosity requires putting others first. If you can do that, giving becomes much easier.

3. Don't Allow the Desire for Possessions to Control You

According to my friend Earle Wilson, people can be divided into three groups: "Haves, have-nots, and have not paid for what they have." More and more people are becoming enslaved to the desire to acquire. Author Richard Foster writes, "Owning things is an obsession in our culture. If we own it, we feel we can control it; and if we can control it, we feel it will give us more pleasure. The idea is an illusion." If you want to be in charge of your heart, don't allow possessions to take charge of you.

4. Regard Money as a Resource

Someone once said that when it comes to money, you can't win. If you focus on making it, you're materialistic. If you try to but don't make any, you're a loser. If you make a lot and keep it, you're a miser. If you make it and spend it, you're a spendthrift. If you don't care about making any, you're unambitious. If you make a lot and still have it when you die, you're a fool—for trying to take it with you.

The only way to really win with money is to hold it

loosely—and be generous with it to accomplish things of value. As E. Stanley Jones said, "Money is a wonderful servant but a terrible master. If it gets on top and you get under it, you will become its slave."

5. Develop the Habit of Giving

In 1889, millionaire industrialist Andrew Carnegie wrote an essay called "Gospel of Wealth." In it he said that the life of a wealthy person should have two periods: a time of acquiring wealth and one of redistributing it. The only way to maintain an attitude of generosity is to make it your habit to give—your time, attention, money, and resources. Richard Foster advises, "Just the very act of letting go of money, or some other treasure, does something within us. It destroys the demon greed." If you're enslaved by greed, you cannot lead.

R E F L E C T I N G   O N   I T

Are you a generous leader? Do you continually look for ways to add value to others? Are you giving money to something greater than yourself? And to whom are you giving your time? Are you pouring your life into others? Are you helping those who cannot help you or give anything in return? Writer John Bunyan affirmed, "You have not lived today until you have done something for someone who can never repay you." If you aren't giving in the small areas of your life, you're probably not as generous a leader as you could be.

BRINGING IT HOME

To improve your generosity, do the following:

- *Give something away.* Find out what kind of hold your possessions have on you. Take something you truly value, think of someone you care about who could benefit from it, and give it to him. If you can do it anonymously, even better.

- *Put your money to work.* If you know someone with the vision to do something really great—something that will positively impact the lives of others—provide resources for him to accomplish it. Put your money to work for something that will outlive you.

- *Find someone to mentor.* Once you reach a certain level in your leadership, the most valuable thing you have to give is yourself. Find someone to pour your life into. Then give him time and resources to become a better leader.

DAILY TAKE-AWAY

When popular French author Dominique Lapierre first traveled to India to do research for a new book, he went in style—in a Rolls-Royce Silver Shadow he had just purchased with a book advance. While he was there, he got what he needed for his book *The City of Joy.* But he also received something else: a passion to help the poor and miserable people he discovered there. That discovery has changed his life forever. Now he divides his time between writing, fund-raising, and donating time and money to help the people. His attitude can be summed up by the words of Indian poet Rabindranath Tagore, which are printed on the back of Lapierre's business card: "All that is not given is lost." What are you currently losing by holding on to it?

INITIATIVE:

YOU WON'T LEAVE HOME WITHOUT IT

Success seems to be connected with action.

Successful people keep moving.

They make mistakes, but they don't quit.

—Conrad Hilton, Hotel Executive

Of all the things a leader should fear,

complacency should head the list.

—John C. Maxwell

JUST ANOTHER STEP FORWARD

Kemmons Wilson has always been an initiator. He started working when he was seven years old and hasn't stopped since. He
began by selling magazines, newspapers, and popcorn. In 1930
at the ripe old age of seventeen, he decided to try a salaried job
for the first time, working for a cotton broker. He made $12 a
week writing figures on the broker's price board.

When a bookkeeper's job paying $35 a week opened up,
Wilson applied for it and got it. But when he received his pay, it
was still only $12. He requested a raise and got one. The next
week he received an additional $3. When he asked why he didn't
get the same $35 as the other bookkeeper, he was told the com-
pany wouldn't pay that kind of money to a seventeen-year-old
kid. Wilson gave his notice. That was the last time in more than
seventy-five years that he took a salaried job.

Wilson made money in a variety of businesses after that: pin-
ball machines, soft drink distribution, and vending machines.
And he was able to save enough money to build his mother a
house. That's when he realized home building had a lot of potential. So he went into the business in Memphis and made a fortune, capitalizing on the postwar building boom.

Wilson's initiative made him a lot of money, but it didn't
make an impact on the world—not until 1951, that is. That was
the year the Memphis businessman took his family on vacation
to Washington, D.C. On that trip, he learned about the sorry
state of hotel lodging in the United States. Motels had sprung up

all over the country since the 1920s. Some were nice family places. Others rented beds by the hour. The problem was a traveler didn't know which he would find.

"You never could tell what you were getting," Wilson recalled later. "Some of the places were too squalid for words. And they all charged for children. That made my Scottish blood boil." A guy like Wilson who had five children really took a beating. Motels charged $4 to $6 a night for a room *plus* $2 per child. It tripled his bill.

Most people would have complained and then forgotten about it. But Wilson, always the initiator, decided to take action and do something about it. "Let's go home and start a chain of family hotels," he said to his wife, "hotels with a name you could trust." His goal was to build four hundred hotels. His wife just laughed.

When Wilson returned to Memphis, he hired a draftsman to help him design his first hotel. He wanted it to be clean, simple, and predictable. And he wanted it to have all the things he and his family had missed, such as a television in every room and a pool. The next year he opened his first hotel on the outskirts of Memphis. Its name flashed out front on a huge fifty-three-foot-tall sign. It was called the Holiday Inn.

It took Wilson longer than he expected to reach four hundred hotels. By 1959, he had one hundred. But when he decided to franchise them, that boosted the openings. By 1964, there were five hundred Holiday Inns. In 1968, there were one thousand. And by 1972, a Holiday Inn opened somewhere in the world every seventy-two hours. The chain was still growing in 1979 when Wilson stepped down from the company's leadership after a heart attack.

"I was so hungry when I was young," Wilson said, "I just had to do something to make a living. And when I retired after my heart attack, I went home to smell the roses. That lasted about a month." It's just too hard for an initiator to stop making things happen.

FLESHING IT OUT

In *The 21 Irrefutable Laws of Leadership,* I pointed out that leaders are responsible for initiating a connection with their followers. But that's not the only area where leaders must show initiative. They must always look for opportunities and be ready to take action.

What qualities do leaders possess that enable them to make things happen? I see at least four.

1. They Know What They Want

Humorous pianist Oscar Levant once joked, "Once I make up my mind, I'm full of indecision." Unfortunately, that's the way many people actually operate. But no one can be both indecisive and effective. As Napoleon Hill says, "The starting point of all achievement is desire." If you are going to be an effective leader, you've got to know what you want. That's the only way you'll recognize opportunity when it comes.

2. They Push Themselves to Act

There's an old saying: "You can if you will." Initiators don't wait for other people to motivate them. They knew it is their responsibility to push themselves beyond their comfort zone. And they make it a regular practice. That's why someone such as President Theodore Roosevelt, one of the great initiating leaders of the twentieth century, was able to say, "There is nothing brilliant or outstanding in my record, except perhaps this one thing: I do the things that I believe ought to be done . . . And when I make up my mind to do a thing, I act."

3. They Take More Risks

When leaders know what they want and can push themselves to act, they still have one more hurdle. That's willingness to take risks. Proactive people always take risks. But one of the reasons good leaders are willing to take risks is that they recognize there is a price for not initiating too. President John F. Kennedy asserted, "There are risks and costs to a program of action, but they are far less than the long-range risks and costs of comfortable inaction."

4. They Make More Mistakes

The good news for initiators is that they make things happen. The bad news is that they make lots of mistakes. IBM founder Thomas J. Watson recognized that when he remarked, "The way to succeed is to double your failure rate."

Even though initiating leaders experience more failure, they don't let it bother them. The greater the potential, the greater the chance for failure. Senator Robert Kennedy summed it up: "Only those who dare to fail greatly can ever achieve greatly." If you want to achieve great things as a leader, you must be willing to initiate and put yourself on the line.

R E F L E C T I N G   O N   I T

Are you an initiator? Are you constantly on the lookout for opportunity, or do you wait for it to come to you? Are you willing to take steps based on your best instincts? Or do you endlessly analyze everything? Former Chrysler chairman Lee Iacocca said, "Even the right decision is the wrong decision if it is made too late." When was the last time you initiated something significant in your life? If you haven't pushed yourself lately and gotten out of your comfort zone, you may need to jump-start your initiative.

B R I N G I N G   I T   H O M E

To improve your initiative, do the following:

- *Change your mind-set.* If you lack initiative, recognize that the problem comes from the inside, not from others. Determine why you hesitate to take action. Does risk scare you? Are you discouraged by past failures? Do you not see the potential that opportunity offers? Find the source of your hesitation, and address it. You won't be able to move forward on the outside until you can move forward on the inside.

- *Don't wait for opportunity to knock.* Opportunity doesn't come to the door knocking. You've got to go out and look for it. Take stock of your assets, talents, and resources. Doing that will give you an idea of your potential. Now, spend every day for a week looking for opportunities. Where do you see needs? Who is looking for expertise you have? What unreached group of people is practically dying for what you have to offer? Opportunity is everywhere.

- *Take the next step.* It's one thing to see opportunity. It's another to do something about it. As someone once quipped, everyone has a great idea in the shower. But only a few people step out, dry off, and do something about it. Pick the best opportunity you see, and take it as far as you can. Don't stop until you've done everything you can to make it happen.

Daily Take-Away

In 1947, Lester Wunderman was arbitrarily fired from his advertising job in New York. But the young man knew he could learn a lot from the head of the agency, Max Sackheim. The next morning, Wunderman went back to his office and worked just as he had before—but without pay.

Sackheim ignored him for a month, but finally walked up to Wunderman and said, "Okay, you win. I never saw a man who wanted a job more than he wanted money."

Wunderman went on to become one of the most successful advertising men of the century. He is known as the father of direct marketing. It will take a bold step from you today to reach your potential tomorrow.

11

LISTENING:

TO CONNECT WITH THEIR HEARTS,

USE YOUR EARS

The ear of the leader
must ring with the voices of the people.

—*Woodrow Wilson, American President*

A good leader encourages followers to tell him
what he needs to know, not what he wants to hear.

—*John C. Maxwell*

As Much as She Talks,
She Listens More

Who would you include in a list of the most influential people in the United States? Certainly the president would make that list. So would Alan Greenspan. Michael Jordan might make it—his is the most recognized face on the planet. You could argue for Bill Gates to be on it. Stop for a moment and think about the people you would include. Now I want you to add a name that you might not have considered: Oprah Winfrey.

In 1985, Winfrey was practically unknown. She appeared in Steven Spielberg's *The Color Purple,* and she was the host of a local morning talk show, which she had been doing in Chicago for a year. What success she had achieved could be attributed to her ability to talk. "Communicating with people is how I always developed any kind of value about myself," explains Winfrey. And she received praise for it early in life. "I remember being two years old and speaking in church and hearing people say, 'That child sure can talk. That is one talking child.'"

But Winfrey also did more than her share of listening. In fact, the ability to listen has been a chief characteristic of her life. She is an inveterate learner, and her listening ability got its start as she absorbed the wisdom of writers. She devoured fiction and biographies, learning about how other people feel and think—and in the process she also learned about herself.

That bent toward listening has served her well in every

aspect of her career. Its application is obvious for her television show. She is constantly observing and listening to find issues to address on the air. And when she brings celebrities, authors, or experts on her show, she genuinely listens to what they have to say. Music star Madonna said about her, "She has been in the public eye for so long, yet she has this amazing rapport with people. I don't know how she does it." She does it through listening.

Oprah Winfrey's ability to listen has been rewarded with remarkable success and incredible influence. She is the highest paid entertainer in the world and is worth nearly half a billion dollars. Each week, thirty-three million people in the United States alone watch her show.

Despite her show's success, she recently gave thought to discontinuing it. But instead she decided to revamp it. How did she decide what changes to make? She asked her staff.

"It doesn't have to be work," she told them. "Making changes in this show is like making changes in our lives. It can be fun to do. So let's stretch. What can we do to make it more fun?"

She had a lot of doubts about one of the ideas her people came up with. But she also had enough wisdom to listen to it— and give it a try. The idea was for a book club. As you probably know, its success has been phenomenal. Hundreds of thousands of people are learning and growing by reading, some for the first time. And Winfrey is delighted. Her goal in life is to add value to people. And she succeeds because she listens.

FLESHING IT OUT

In *The 21 Irrefutable Laws of Leadership,* I point out that leaders touch a heart before they ask for a hand. That's the Law of Connection. But before a leader can touch a person's heart, he has to know what's in it. He learns that by listening.

An unwillingness to listen is too common among poor leaders. Peter Drucker, the father of American management, believes that 60 percent of all management problems are the result of faulty communications. I would say that the overwhelming majority of communication problems come from poor listening.

A lot of voices are clamoring out there for your attention. As you think about how to spend your listening time, keep in mind that you have two purposes for listening: to connect with people and to learn. For that reason, you should keep your ear open to these people:

1. Your Followers
Good leaders, the kind that people want to follow, do more than conduct business when they interact with followers. They take the time to get a feel for who each one is as a person. Philip Stanhope, the earl of Chesterfield, believed, "many a man would rather you heard his story than granted his request." If you're in the habit of listening only to the facts and not the person who expresses them, change your focus—and really listen.

2. *Your Customers*

A Cherokee saying states, "Listen to the whispers and you won't have to hear the screams." I am amazed by the leaders who are so caught up in their own ideas that they never hear their customers' concerns, complaints, and suggestions. In his book *Business @ the Speed of Thought,* Microsoft CEO Bill Gates said, "Unhappy customers are always a concern. They're also your greatest opportunity." Good leaders always make it a priority to keep in contact with the people they're serving.

3. *Your Competitors*

Sam Markewich announced, "If you don't agree with me, it means you haven't been listening." Though he was no doubt making a joke, the sad truth is that when a leader sees another organization as competition, he focuses his attention on building his own case or championing his cause and forgets to learn from what the other group is doing.

Larry King says, "I remind myself every morning: nothing I say this day will teach me anything. So if I'm going to learn, I must do it by listening." As a leader, you don't want to base your actions on what the other guy is doing, but you should still listen and learn what you can to improve yourself.

4. *Your Mentors*

No leader is so advanced or experienced that he can afford to be without a mentor. I've learned so much from leaders who have more experience than I have, people such as Melvin Maxwell (my father), Elmer Towns, Jack Hayford, Fred Smith, and J. Oswald Sanders. If you don't already have a mentor, go out and find one. If you can't get someone to help you in person, begin the process by reading books. That's where I got started. The main thing is to get the process under way.

REFLECTING ON IT

Are you a good listener? I know when I started in leadership, I wasn't. I was too busy doing my own thing and trying to make things happen. But once I slowed down and paid greater attention to what was going on around me, I found that my activity had sharper focus and accomplished more.

When was the last time you really paid close attention to people and what they have to say? Do more than just grab onto facts. Start listening not only for words, but also for feelings, meanings, and undercurrents.

BRINGING IT HOME

To improve your listening, do the following:

- *Change your schedule.* Do you spend time listening to your followers, customers, competitors, and mentors? If you don't have all four groups on your calendar regularly, you're probably not giving them enough attention. Pencil in time for each of them on a daily, weekly, or monthly basis.

• *Meet people on their turf.* A key to being a good listener is to find common ground with people. The next time you meet with an employee or a customer, discipline yourself to ask four or five questions about him as a person. Get to know who he is, and seek common ground to build your connection with him.

• *Listen between the lines.* As you interact with people, you certainly want to pay attention to the factual content of the conversation. But don't ignore the emotional content. Sometimes you can learn more about what's really going on by reading between the lines. Spend time in the coming days and weeks listening with your heart.

DAILY TAKE-AWAY

President Theodore Roosevelt was a man of action, but he was also a good listener, and he appreciated that quality in other people. Once at a gala ball, he grew tired of meeting people who returned his remarks with stiff, mindless pleasantries. So he began to greet people with a smile, saying, "I murdered my grandmother this morning." Most people, so nervous about meeting him, didn't even hear what he said. But one diplomat did. Upon hearing the president's remark, he leaned over and whispered to him, "I'm sure she had it coming to her!" The only way to find out what you're missing is to start listening.

Passion:

Take This Life and Love It

When a leader reaches out in passion,
he is usually met with an answering passion.

—John C. Maxwell

Anyone can dabble, but once you've made that
commitment, your blood has that particular thing in it,
and it's very hard for people to stop you.

—Bill Cosby, Comedian

PIZZA SAUCE IS IN HIS BLOOD

In *The 21 Irrefutable Laws of Leadership,* I tell the story of Papa John's Pizza and how the company, founded in 1984 by John Schnatter, grew from 1 to 46 stores in its first seven years and then from 46 to 1,600 in the seven years after that. The phenomenal success the company experienced in the second half was due to the Law of Explosive Growth, which says, "To add growth, lead followers—to multiply, lead leaders." But what was the key to Papa John's success in the first half?

The answer is passion. John Schnatter not only eats Papa John's Pizza; he breathes, sleeps, and lives it. It is always his predominating thought. Lehman Brothers analyst Michael Speiser said of him in *Success* magazine, "Pizza is Schnatter's life, and he takes it very seriously."

Schnatter's philosophy is simple and straightforward. "Concentrate on what you do well," he advises, "and do it better than anybody else." What he does well is lead the fastest-growing business of its kind in the world. And he enjoys it so much that he is always in the thick of things.

Recently he went to visit a franchise owned by his wife, Annette, in downtown Louisville and found that the store was unexpectedly swamped with orders. What did he do? He jumped in and helped make pizzas for an hour and a half. It's something he loves doing. He visits stores four or five times a week—often unannounced—just to make sure everything is on track.

"Talking about my dreams for a pizza business at age twenty-two, people thought I was crazy," Schnatter has said. "Vendors, bankers and even some friends just laughed when I told them I'd be opening five or six stores a month." Now he regularly opens an amazing *thirty* stores a month—a new store every day of the year.

And he wants to increase that. A franchise opened in Mexico, and Schnatter has plans to expand into Venezuela, Puerto Rico, and other foreign markets. He doesn't intend to stop until he leads the largest seller of pizza in the world. He just might do it because he loves it and gives it everything he's got.

F L E S H I N G   I T   O U T

Experts spend a lot of time trying to figure out what makes people successful. They often look at people's credentials, intelligence, education, and other factors. But more than anything else, passion makes the difference. David Sarnoff of RCA maintains that "nobody can be successful unless he loves his work."

If you look at the lives of effective leaders, you will find that they often don't fit into a stereotypical mold. For example, more than 50 percent of all CEOs of Fortune 500 companies had C or C– averages in college. Nearly 75 percent of all U.S. presidents were in the bottom half of their school classes. And more than 50 percent of all millionaire entrepreneurs never finished college. What makes it possible for people who might seem ordinary to achieve great things? The answer is passion. Nothing can take the place of passion in a leader's life.

Take a look at four truths about passion and what it can do for you as a leader:

1. Passion Is the First Step to Achievement

Your desire determines your destiny. Think of great leaders, and you will be struck by their passion: Gandhi for human rights, Winston Churchill for freedom, Martin Luther King Jr. for equality, Bill Gates for technology.

Anyone who lives beyond an ordinary life has great desire. It's true in any field: weak desire brings weak results, just as a small fire creates little heat. The stronger your fire, the greater the desire—and the greater the potential.

2. Passion Increases Your Willpower

It is said that a dispassionate young man approached the Greek philosopher Socrates and casually stated, "O great Socrates, I come to you for knowledge."

The philosopher took the young man down to the sea, waded in with him, and then dunked him under the water for thirty seconds. When he let the young man up for air, Socrates asked him to repeat what he wanted.

"Knowledge, O great one," he sputtered. Socrates put him under the water again, only that time a little longer. After repeated dunkings and responses, the philosopher asked, "What do you want?" The young man finally gasped, "Air. I want air!"

"Good," answered Socrates. "Now, when you want knowledge as much as you wanted air, you shall have it."

There is no substitute for passion. It is fuel for the will. If you want anything badly enough, you can find the willpower to achieve it. The only way to have that kind of desire is to develop passion.

3. Passion Changes You

If you follow your passion—instead of others' perceptions—you can't help becoming a more dedicated, productive person. And that increases your ability to impact others. In the end, your passion will have more influence than your personality.

4. Passion Makes the Impossible Possible

Human beings are so made that whenever anything fires the soul, impossibilities vanish. A fire in the heart lifts everything in your life. That's why passionate leaders are so effective. A leader with great passion and few skills always outperforms a leader with great skills and no passion.

REFLECTING ON IT

Despite the power of passion, many people in our culture seem to believe that passion is something to be suspicious about. Sociologist Tony Campolo has observed, "We are caught up at a particular stage in our national ethos in which we're not only materialistic but worse than that; we're becoming emotionally dead as people. We don't sing, we don't dance, we don't even commit sin with much enthusiasm."

Is passion a characteristic of your life? Do you wake up feeling enthusiastic about your day? Is the first day of the week your favorite, or do you live from weekend to weekend, sleepwalking through your everyday routine? How long has it been since you couldn't sleep because you were too *excited* by an idea?

If passion is not a quality in your life, you're in trouble as a leader. The truth is that you can never lead something you don't care passionately about. You can't start a fire in your organization unless one is first burning in you.

BRINGING IT HOME

To increase your passion, do the following:

- *Take your temperature.* How passionate are you about your life and work? Does it show? Get an honest assessment by querying several coworkers and your spouse about your level of desire. You won't become passionate until you believe passion can be the difference maker in your life.

- *Return to your first love.* Many people allow life and its circumstances to get them off track. Think back to when you were just starting out in your career—or even farther back to when you were a child. What really turned your crank? What could you spend hours and hours doing? Try to recapture your old enthusiasm. Then evaluate your life and career in light of those old loves.

- *Associate with people of passion.* It sounds hokey, but birds of a feather really do flock together. If you've lost your fire, get around some firelighters. Passion is contagious. Schedule some time with people who can infect you with it.

DAILY TAKE-AWAY

General Billy Mitchell, a career army officer, was assigned to an aviation section in 1916. That's where he learned to fly, and it became the passion of his life. Though aircraft played a minor role in World War I, he could see the military potential of air power. After the war, he began a campaign to convince the military to create an air force. He provided demonstration after demonstration of what airplanes could do, but he met strong resistance. Frustrated, he forced the army to court-martial him in 1925. A year later he resigned. Only after World War II was Mitchell exonerated—and posthumously awarded the Medal of Honor. He was willing to pay any price to do what he knew was right. How about you?

POSITIVE ATTITUDE:

IF YOU BELIEVE YOU CAN, YOU CAN

The greatest discovery of my generation
is that human beings can alter their lives by
altering their attitude of mind.

—*William James, Psychologist*

A successful man is one who can lay a firm foundation
with the bricks others have thrown at him.

—*David Brinkley, Television Journalist*

M O R E   T H A N   P E R S P I R A T I O N
A N D   I N S P I R A T I O N

Life magazine named him the number one man of the millennium. The number of things he invented is astounding—1,093. He held more patents than any other person in the world, having been granted at least one every year for sixty-five consecutive years. He also developed the modern research laboratory. His name was Thomas Edison.

Most people credit Edison's ability to creative genius. He credited it to hard work. "Genius," he declared, "is ninety-nine percent perspiration and one percent inspiration." I believe his success was also the result of a third factor: his positive attitude.

Edison was an optimist who saw the best in everything. "If we did all the things we were capable of doing," he once said, "we would literally astound ourselves." When it took him ten thousand tries to find the right materials for the incandescent light bulb, he didn't see them as that many failures. With each attempt he gained information about what didn't work, bringing him closer to a solution. He never doubted that he would find a good one. His belief could be summarized by his statement: "Many of life's failures are people who did not realize how close they were to success when they gave up."

Probably the most notable display of Edison's positive attitude can be seen in the way he approached a tragedy that occurred when he was in his late sixties. The lab he had built in West Orange, New Jersey, was world famous. He called the

fourteen-building complex his invention factory. Its main building was massive—greater than three football fields in size. From
that base of operations, he and his staff conceived of inventions,
developed prototypes, manufactured products, and shipped
them to customers. It became a model for modern research and
manufacturing.

Edison loved the place. He spent every minute he could
there. He even slept there, often on one of the lab tables. But on
a December day in 1914, his beloved lab caught fire. As he stood
outside and watched it burn, he is reported to have said, "Kids,
go get your mother. She'll never see another fire like this one."

Most people would have been crushed. Not Edison. "I am
sixty-seven," he stated after the tragedy, "but not too old to make
a fresh start. I've been through a lot of things like this." He
rebuilt the lab, and he kept working for another seventeen years.
"I am long on ideas, but short on time," he commented. "I expect
to live to be only about a hundred." He died at age eighty-four.

FLESHING IT OUT

If Edison hadn't been such a positive person, he never would
have achieved such success as an inventor. If you look at the lives
of people in any profession who achieve lasting success, you will
find that they almost always possess a positive outlook on life.

If you desire to be an effective leader, having a positive attitude is essential. It not only determines your level of contentment
as a person, but it also has an impact on how others interact

with you. To learn more about what it means to be positive, think on these things:

1. Your Attitude Is a Choice

The average person wants to wait for someone else to motivate him. He perceives that his circumstances are responsible for the way he thinks. But which comes first—the attitude or the circumstances? That's really a chicken-or-the-egg kind of question. The truth is that it doesn't matter which came first. No matter what happened to you yesterday, your attitude is your choice today.

Psychologist Victor Frankl believed, "The last of our human freedoms is to choose our attitude in any given circumstances." He knew the truth of that statement. Frankl survived imprisonment in a Nazi death camp, and throughout his ordeal, he wouldn't allow his attitude to deteriorate. If he could maintain a good attitude, so can you.

2. Your Attitude Determines Your Actions

Family life expert Denis Waitley addresses this issue: "The winner's edge is not in a gifted birth, a high IQ, or in talent. The winner's edge is all in the attitude, not aptitude. Attitude is the criterion for success." Your attitude is crucial because it determines how you act.

3. Your People Are a Mirror of Your Attitude

I am constantly amazed by people who display a poor attitude, yet expect their people to be upbeat. But the Law of Magnetism really is true: who you are is who you attract.

If you look at Edison's life, you can see that his positive attitude and enthusiasm not only fueled him but also inspired his people to keep pressing on until they succeeded. He purposely tried to pass on that quality to others. He once remarked, "If the only thing we leave our kids is the quality of enthusiasm, we will have given them an estate of incalculable value."

4. Maintaining a Good Attitude Is Easier Than Regaining One

In *Earth and Altar,* Eugene H. Peterson wrote, "Pity is one of the noblest emotions available to human beings; self-pity is possibly the most ignoble . . . [It] is an incapacity, a crippling emotional disease that severely distorts our perception of reality . . . a narcotic that leaves its addicts wasted and derelict."

If you already have a positive attitude, I want to encourage you to keep it up. On the other hand, if you have a difficult time expecting the best of yourself and others, don't despair. Because you choose your attitude, you can change it.

REFLECTING ON IT

English heart surgeon Martyn Lloyd-Jones asserted, "Most unhappiness in life is due to the fact that you are listening to yourself rather than talking to yourself." What kind of voices do you hear? When you meet people, do you tell yourself they'll let you down? When you face new experiences, does a voice in your head say you're going to fail? If you're hearing negative messages, you need to learn to give yourself positive mental pep talks. The best way to retrain your attitude is to prevent your mind from going down any negative forks in the road.

BRINGING IT HOME

To improve your attitude, do the following:

- *Feed yourself the right "food."* If you've been starved of anything positive, then you need to start feeding yourself a regular diet of motivational material. Read books that encourage a positive attitude. Listen to motivational tapes. The more negative you are, the longer it will take to turn your attitude around. But if you consume a steady diet of the right "food," you can become a positive thinker.

- *Achieve a goal every day.* Some people get into a rut of negativity because they feel they're not making progress. If that describes you, then begin setting achievable daily goals for yourself. A pattern of positive achievement will help you develop a pattern of positive thinking.

- *Write it on your wall.* We all need reminders to help us keep thinking right. Alex Haley used to keep a picture in his office of a turtle on a fence post to remind him that everybody needed the help of others. As incentive, people put up awards they've won, inspirational posters, or letters they've received. Find something that will work for you and put it on your wall.

DAILY TAKE-AWAY

When you look at any professional athlete, you see great talent. But the mind is what elevates the best to the highest level. For example, look at Chris Evert. One of the greatest female athletes of all time, she holds 18 grand slam titles and an overall win-loss record of 1,309 and 146. In her seventeen-year career, she never ranked below number four. She commented, "The thing that separates good players from great ones is mental attitude. It might only make a difference of two or three points in an entire match but how you play those key points often makes the difference between winning and losing. If the mind is strong you can do almost anything you want." Is your mind "conditioned" to win the key points ahead of you?

PROBLEM SOLVING:

YOU CAN'T LET YOUR PROBLEMS

BE A PROBLEM

You can measure a leader by the problems he tackles.
He always looks for ones his own size.

—*John C. Maxwell*

The measure of success is not
whether you have a tough problem to deal with,
but whether it is the same problem you had last year.

—*John Foster Dulles, Former Secretary of State*

THE SMALL-TOWN MERCHANT
WHO COULD

The founder of Wal-Mart, Sam Walton, has been called many things, including enemy of small-town America and destroyer of Main Street merchants. "Quite a few smaller stores have gone out of business during the time of Wal-Mart's growth," conceded Walton. "Some people have tried to turn it into this big controversy, sort of a 'Save the Small Town Merchants' deal, like they were whales or whooping cranes or something." The truth is that Walton *was* a small-town, Main Street merchant of the type he is criticized for displacing. The only difference is that he was an excellent leader who was able to solve problems and change rather than go out of business.

Sam Walton was born in Kingfisher, Oklahoma, and grew up in Columbia, Missouri. He demonstrated leadership in high school when he was elected student-body president, led his football team to an undefeated season and state championship as its quarterback, and then performed the same feat with the basketball team as its five-foot-nine-inch floor leader.

After graduating from college and working for a few years, Walton served in the army during World War II. When he got out, he selected a career in retail, the field he loved, and along with his wife picked the small town of Bentonville, Arkansas, in which to live. That's where they opened a Walton's Five and Dime Variety Store.

The business did well, partly because of Walton's hustle, but also because he had shown foresight in making his store self-service, a new concept at the time. He worked hard and continued to expand. By 1960, he had fifteen stores. But that was also about the time when competitor Herb Gibson brought discount stores into northwest Arkansas. They competed directly with Walton's variety stores.

"We really had only two choices," said Walton, "stay in the variety store business and be hit hard by the discounting wave, or open a discount store. So I started running all over the country, studying the concept . . . We opened Wal-Mart Number 1 on July 2, 1962, in Rogers, Arkansas, right down the road from Bentonville."

Walton soon added additional stores. His Wal-Mart chain was small compared to some of the others begun around the same time—Kmart, Target, and Woolco—but it was going strong. And that led to the next problem. Walton realized that he needed to improve the stores' planning and distribution. He and his people solved the problem by creating central distribution centers. That, along with computerization, allowed them to order in bulk, keep track of each store's needs, and distribute to them quickly and efficiently. And when the outlay for new equipment and buildings for the new distribution centers created a heavy debt load, it was merely another problem to be solved. Walton did it by taking the company public in 1970.

When he died in 1992, the company operated more than 1,700 stores in forty-two states and Mexico. Sam Walton, the small-town variety store owner, had become America's number one retailer. And since his death, the company has continued strongly, its leadership still solving problems as they arise and keeping Wal-Mart and the other retail chain, Sam's Club, moving forward.

FLESHING IT OUT

Effective leaders, like Sam Walton, always rise to a challenge. That's one of the things that separates winners from whiners. While other retailers complained about the competition, Walton rose above it by solving his problems with creativity and tenacity.

No matter what field a leader is in, he will face problems. They are inevitable for three reasons. First, we live in a world of growing complexity and diversity. Second, we interact with people. And third, we cannot control all the situations we face.

Leaders with good problem-solving ability demonstrate five qualities:

1. They Anticipate Problems
Since problems are inevitable, good leaders anticipate them. Anyone who expects the road to be easy will continually find himself in trouble. I heard a story about David Livingstone, the missionary to Africa, that illustrates the kind of attitude leaders need. A mission organization wanted to send helpers to Dr. Livingstone, so its leader wrote, "Have you found a good road to where you are? If so, we want to send other men to join you."

Livingstone replied, "If you have men who will come *only* if they know there is a good road, I don't want them. I want men who will come even if there is no road at all." If you keep your attitude positive but plan for the worst, you'll find yourself in a good position to solve problems that come your way.

2. They Accept the Truth

People respond to problems in these ways: they refuse to accept them; they accept them and then put up with them; or they accept them and try to make things better. Leaders must always do the latter.

Broadcaster Paul Harvey said, "In times like these it is good to remember that there have always been times like these." No leader can simultaneously have his head in the sand and navigate his people through troubled waters. Effective leaders face up to the reality of a situation.

3. They See the Big Picture

Leaders must continually see the big picture. They cannot afford to be overwhelmed by emotion. Nor can they allow themselves to get so bogged down in the details that they lose sight of what's important. Author Alfred Armand Montapert wrote, "The majority see the obstacles; the few see the objectives; history records the successes of the latter, while oblivion is the reward of the former."

4. They Handle One Thing at a Time

Richard Sloma has this advice: "Never try to solve all the problems at once—make them line up for you one-by-one." The leaders who get into trouble most often are the ones who are overwhelmed by the sheer size or volume of their troubles and then dabble at problem solving. If you're faced with lots of problems, make sure you really solve the one you're working on before moving on to the next one.

5. They Don't Give Up a Major Goal When They're Down

Effective leaders understand the peak-to-peak principle. They make major decisions when they are experiencing a positive swing in their leadership, not during the dark times. As NFL fullback Bob Christian says, "I never decide whether it's time to retire during training camp." He knows not to give up when he is in the valley.

REFLECTING ON IT

Author George Matthew Adams stated, "What you think means more than anything else in your life. More than what you earn, more than where you live, more than your social position, and more than what anyone else may think about you." Every problem introduces you to yourself. It shows you how you think and what you're made of.

When you come face-to-face with a problem, how do you react? Do you ignore it and hope it will go away? Do you feel powerless to solve it? Have you had such bad experiences trying to solve problems in the past that you've just given up? Or do you tackle them willingly? The ability to solve problems effectively comes from experience facing and overcoming obstacles. Each time you solve another problem, you get a little better at the process. But if you never try, fail, and try again, you'll never be good at it.

BRINGING IT HOME

To improve your problem solving, do the following:

- *Look for trouble.* If you've been avoiding problems, go out looking for them. You'll only get better if you gain experience dealing with them. Find situations that need fixing, come up with several viable solutions, and then take them to a leader with good problem-solving experience. You'll learn from his decisions how he thinks when handling difficulties.

- *Develop a method.* Some people have a hard time solving problems because they don't know how to tackle them. Try using the TEACH process:

  T IME—spend time to discover the real issue.

  E XPOSURE—find out what others have done.

  A SSISTANCE—have your team study all angles.

  C REATIVITY—brainstorm multiple solutions.

  H IT IT—implement the best solution.

- *Surround yourself with problem solvers.* If you aren't a good problem solver, bring others onto your team who are. They will immediately complement your weaknesses, and you will also learn from them.

DAILY TAKE-AWAY

Boxer Gene Tunney won the world heavyweight championship by beating Jack Dempsey. Most people don't know that when Tunney started his boxing career, he was a power puncher. But before turning pro, he broke both hands. His doctor and manager told him he would never be a world champion as a result. But that didn't deter him.

"If I can't become a champion as a puncher," he said, "I'll make it as a boxer." He learned and he became one of the most skillful boxers ever to become champion. Never allow others to put obstacles in the pathway to your dreams.

15

RELATIONSHIPS:
IF YOU GET ALONG, THEY'LL GO ALONG

The most important single ingredient
in the formula of success is knowing how
to get along with people.

—Theodore Roosevelt, American President

People don't care how much you know,
until they know how much you care.

—John C. Maxwell

THE BEST MEDICINE

If you're not a physician, you've probably never heard the name William Osler. He was a doctor, university professor, and author who practiced medicine and taught until his death at age seventy in 1919. His book, *Principles and Practice of Medicine,* influenced the preparation of physicians for more than forty years in the entire English-speaking world, China, and Japan. Yet that was not his greatest contribution to the world. Osler worked on putting the human heart back into the practice of medicine.

Osler's penchant for leadership became apparent while he was still a child. He was a natural ringleader and the most influential student in his school. He always showed an uncanny ability with people. Everything Osler did spoke to the importance of building relationships. As he grew older and became a doctor, he founded the Association of American Physicians so that medical professionals could come together, share information, and support one another. As a teacher, he changed the way medical schools functioned. He brought students out of dry lecture halls and into the hospital wards to interact with patients. He believed that students learn first and best from the patients themselves.

But Osler's passion was to teach doctors compassion. He told a group of medical students,

> There is a strong feeling abroad among people—you see it in the newspapers—that we doctors are given over now- adays to science; that we care much more for the disease

and its scientific aspects than for the individual . . . I would urge upon you in your own practice, to care more particularly for the individual patient . . . Dealing as we do with poor suffering humanity, we see the man unmasked, exposed to all the frailties and weaknesses, and you have to keep your heart soft and tender lest you have too great a contempt for your fellow creatures.

Osler's ability to show compassion and build relationships can be capsulized by his treatment of a patient during the 1918 epidemic of influenzal pneumonia. Osler usually limited his work to hospitals, but because of the magnitude of the epidemic, he treated many patients in their homes. The mother of a little girl recounted how Osler visited her child twice a day, speaking to her gently and playing with her to entertain her and gather information about her symptoms.

Knowing the child was nearing death, Osler arrived one day with a beautiful red rose wrapped in paper, the last rose of the summer, grown in his own garden. He presented it to her, explaining that even roses couldn't stay as long as they wanted in one place, but had to go to a new home. The child seemed to take comfort from his words and the gift. She died a few days later.

Osler died the next year. One of his British colleagues said of him,

So passed into history, untimely, even though he had attained unto the allotted span, the greatest physician in history . . .

And above all it is as a friend that during his lifetime we regarded Osler; as one who possessed the genius of friendship to a greater degree than anyone of our generations. It was his wonderful interest in all of us that was the outstanding feature . . . It was from his humanity, his extraordinary interest in his fellows, that all his other powers seemed to flow.

FLESHING IT OUT

The ability to work with people and develop relationships is absolutely indispensable to effective leadership. According to the May 1991 issue of *Executive Female* magazine, a survey was taken of employers asking for the top three traits they desired in employees. Number one on the list was the ability to relate to people: 84 percent responded that they sought good interpersonal skills. Only 40 percent listed education and experience in their top three. And if *employees* need good people skills, think about how much more critical those skills are for *leaders*. People truly do want to go along with people they get along with. And while someone can have people skills and not be a good leader, he cannot be a good leader without people skills.

What can a person do to manage and cultivate good relationships as a leader? It requires three things:

1. Have a Leader's Head—Understand People
The first quality of a relational leader is the ability to understand how people feel and think. As you work with others, recognize

that all people, whether leaders or followers, have some things in common:

They like to feel special, so sincerely compliment them.
They want a better tomorrow, so show them hope.
They desire direction, so navigate for them.
They are selfish, so speak to their needs first.
They get low emotionally, so encourage them.
They want success, so help them win.

Recognizing these truths, a leader must still be able to treat people as individuals. The ability to look at each person, understand him, and connect with him is a major factor in relational success. That means treating people differently, not all the same as one another. Marketing expert Rod Nichols notes that in business, this is particularly important: "If you deal with every customer in the same way, you will only close 25 percent to 30 percent of your contacts, because you will only close one personality type. But if you learn how to effectively work with all four personality types, you can conceivably close 100 percent of your contacts."

This sensitivity can be called the soft factor in leadership. You have to be able to adapt your leadership style to the person you're leading.

2. Have a Leader's Heart—Love People

President and CEO of Difinitive Computer Services Henry Gruland captures this idea: "Being a leader is more than just wanting to lead. Leaders have empathy for others and a keen ability to find the best in people . . . not the worst . . . by truly caring for others."

You cannot be a truly effective leader, the kind that people *want* to follow, unless you love people. Physicist Albert Einstein put it this way: "Strange is our situation here upon earth. Each of us comes for a short visit, not knowing why, yet sometimes seeming to divine a purpose. From the standpoint of daily life, however, there is one thing we do know: that man is here for the sake of other men."

3. Extend a Leader's Hand—Help People

Le Roy H. Kurtz of General Motors said, "The fields of industry are strewn with the bones of those organizations whose leadership became infested with dryrot, who believed in taking instead of giving . . . who didn't realize that the only assets that could not be replaced easily were the human ones." People respect a leader who keeps their interests in mind. If your focus is on what you can put into people rather than what you can get out of them, they'll love and respect you—and these create a great foundation for building relationships.

REFLECTING ON IT

How are your people skills? Do you mix well with strangers? Do you interact well with all kinds of people? Can you find common ground readily? What about long-term interaction? Are you able to sustain relationships? If your relational skills are weak, your leadership will always suffer.

To improve your relationships, do the following:

- *Improve your mind.* If your ability to understand people needs improvement, jump-start it by reading several books on the subject. I recommend works written by Dale Carnegie, Alan Loy McGinnis, and Les Parrott III. Then spend more time observing people and talking to them to apply what you've learned.

- *Strengthen your heart.* If you're not as caring toward others as you could be, you need to get the focus off yourself. Make a list of little things you could do to add value to friends and colleagues. Then try to do one of them every day. Don't wait until you feel like it to help others. Act your way into feeling.

- *Repair a hurting relationship.* Think of a valued long-term relationship that has faded. Do what you can to rebuild it. Get in touch with the person and try to reconnect. If you had a falling out, take responsibility for your part in it, and apologize. Try to better understand, love, and serve that person.

DAILY TAKE-AWAY

In a short story titled "The Capitol of the World," Nobel prize-winning author Ernest Hemingway tells about a father and a teenage son, Paco, whose relationship breaks down. After the son runs away from home, the father begins a long journey in search of him. Finally as a last resort, the man puts an ad in the local newspaper in Madrid. It reads, "Dear Paco, meet me in front of the newspaper office tomorrow at noon . . . all is forgiven . . . I love you." The next morning in front of the newspaper office were eight hundred men named Paco, desiring to restore a broken relationship. Never underestimate the power of relationships on people's lives.

RESPONSIBILITY:
IF YOU WON'T CARRY THE BALL,
YOU CAN'T LEAD THE TEAM

Success on any major scale requires you
to accept responsibility . . . In the final analysis,
the one quality that all successful people have
is the ability to take on responsibility.

—*Michael Korda,*
Editor-in-chief of Simon & Schuster

A leader can give up anything—
except final responsibility.

—*John C. Maxwell*

THE ALAMO REVISITED

In late 1835, a group of Texas rebels lay siege to a small mission-turned-fort in San Antonio, Texas. By the end of the year, the Mexican soldiers in it surrendered and headed south, leaving the fort in the rebels' hands. The name of the old church building was the Alamo.

That action set the stage for one of the great heroic events in United States history. The battle that occurred there in February and March of the following year is a story of valor and incredible responsibility.

The battle at the Alamo between American settlers and the Mexican army was inevitable. For twenty-five years, the citizens of Texas repeatedly attempted to gain their independence from the Mexican government. And each time Mexican troops were promptly dispatched to suppress the rebellion. But this time it was different. The fort was manned by a resolute group of 183 volunteers, including seasoned soldiers and frontiersmen William Travis, Davy Crockett, and Jim Bowie. Their motto was "Victory or Death."

In late February, several thousand Mexican soldiers under the command of Antonio Lopez de Santa Anna marched on San Antonio and lay siege to the Alamo. When the Mexicans offered them terms for surrender, the rebel defenders held firm. And when the enemy told them they would be given no quarter if they fought, the Americans would not be moved.

When it became certain that battle was inevitable, the

Texans sent a young man out to try to bring back reinforcements from the Texas army. His name was James Bonham. He slipped out of the old mission at night and made his way ninety-five miles to Goliad for help. But when he arrived, he was told that no troops were available.

For eleven days Santa Anna pounded away at the Alamo. And on the morning of March 6, 1836, the Mexican army stormed the old mission. At the end of the battle, not a single man of the 183 defenders lived. But they had managed to take six hundred enemy soldiers to the grave with them.

And what happened to James Bonham, the messenger who had been sent to Goliad? It would have been easy for Bonham to simply ride away. But his sense of responsibility was too great. Instead he rode back to the Alamo, made his way through enemy lines, and joined his comrades so that he could stand, fight, and die with them.

Though the Americans were defeated at the Alamo, that battle was the turning point in the war with Mexico. "Remember the Alamo" became the cry in subsequent battles, rallying support against General Santa Anna and his troops. Less than two months later, Texas secured its independence.

FLESHING IT OUT

Rarely in American culture today do you see the kind of responsibility displayed by James Bonham and his companions. People now focus more on their rights than on their responsibilities.

Reflecting on current attitudes, my friend Haddon Robinson observes, "If you want to get rich, invest in victimization. It is America's fastest growing industry." He points out that millions of people are becoming rich by identifying, representing, interviewing, treating, insuring, and counseling victims.

Good leaders never embrace a victim mentality. They recognize that who and where they are remain their responsibility—not that of their parents, their spouses, their children, the government, their bosses, or their coworkers. They face whatever life throws at them and give it their best, knowing that they will get an opportunity to lead the team only if they've proved that they can carry the ball.

Take a look at the following characteristics of people who embrace responsibility:

1. They Get the Job Done

In a study of self-made millionaires, Dr. Thomas Stanley of the University of Georgia found that they all have one thing in common: they work hard. One millionaire was asked why he worked twelve to fourteen hours a day. He answered, "It took me fifteen years, working for a large organization, to realize that in our society you work eight hours a day for survival, and if you work only eight hours a day, all you do is survive . . . Everything over eight hours is an investment in your future." No one can do the minimum and reach his maximum potential.

How do people maintain a get-it-done attitude? They think of themselves as self-employed. If you want to achieve more and build your credibility with followers, adopt that mind-set. It can take you far.

2. They Are Willing to Go the Extra Mile
Responsible people never protest, "That's not my job." They're willing to do whatever it takes to complete the work needed by the organization. If you want to succeed, be willing to put the organization ahead of your agenda.

3. They Are Driven by Excellence
Excellence is a great motivator. People who desire excellence— and work hard to achieve it—are almost always responsible. And when they give their all, they live at peace. Success expert Jim Rohn says, "Stress comes from doing less than you can." Make high quality your goal, and responsibility will naturally follow.

4. They Produce Regardless of the Situation
The ultimate quality of a responsible person is the ability to finish. In *An Open Road,* Richard L. Evans writes, "It is priceless to find a person who will take responsibility, who will finish and follow through to the final detail—to know when someone has accepted an assignment that it will be effectively, conscientiously completed." If you want to lead, you've got to produce.

R E F L E C T I N G   O N   I T

Gilbert Arland offers this advice: "When an archer misses the mark he turns and looks for the fault within himself. Failure to hit the bull's-eye is never the fault of the target. To improve your aim, improve yourself."

Are you on target when it comes to responsibility? Do others see you as a finisher? Do people look to you to carry the ball in pressure situations? Are you known for excellence? If you haven't been performing at the highest level, you may need to cultivate a stronger sense of responsibility.

Bringing It Home

To improve your responsibility, do the following:

- *Keep hanging in there.* Sometimes an inability to deliver despite difficult circumstances can be due to a persistence problem. The next time you find yourself in a situation where you're going to miss a deadline, lose a deal, or fail to get a program off the ground, stop and figure out how to succeed. Think outside the lines. Can you work through the night? Can you call a colleague to help you? Can you hire a staff member or find a volunteer to help? Creativity can bring responsibility to life.

- *Admit what's not good enough.* If you have trouble achieving excellence, maybe you've lowered your standards. Look at your personal life for places where you've let things slip. Then make changes to set higher standards. It will help you to reset the bar of excellence for yourself.

- *Find better tools*. If you find that your standards are high, your attitude is good, and you consistently work hard—and you still don't achieve the way you'd like—get better equipped. Improve your skills by taking classes, reading books, and listening to tapes. Find a mentor. Do whatever it takes to become better at what you do.

D A I L Y   T A K E - A W A Y

An inmate at Butte County Jail in California explained his absence from jail to sheriff's deputies in this way: "I was playing pole vault and I got too close to the wall and I fell over the wall. When I regained my senses, I ran around to try and find a way back in, but being unfamiliar with the area, got lost. Next thing I knew I was in Chico." People seldom realize how weak *their* excuses are until they hear some from others.

17

SECURITY:

COMPETENCE NEVER COMPENSATES

FOR INSECURITY

You can't lead people if you need people.

—John C. Maxwell

No man will make a great leader
who wants to do it all himself or get
all the credit for doing it.

—Andrew Carnegie, Industrialist

A C O N S T I T U T I O N O F I R O N A N D
S E C U R I T Y T O M A T C H

During the term of President Ronald Reagan, leaders of seven industrial nations were meeting at the White House to discuss economic policy. Reagan has recounted that during the meeting he came across Canadian Prime Minister Pierre Trudeau strongly upbraiding British Prime Minister Margaret Thatcher, telling her that she was all wrong and that her policies wouldn't work. She stood there in front of him with her head up, listening until he was finished. Then she walked away.

Following the confrontation, Reagan went up to her and said, "Maggie, he should never have spoken to you like that. He was out of line, just entirely out of line. Why did you let him get away with that?"

Thatcher looked at Reagan and answered, "A woman must know when a man is being simply childish."

That story surely typifies Margaret Thatcher. It takes a strong, secure person to succeed as a world leader. And that is especially true when the person is a woman.

Margaret Thatcher has continually swum upstream throughout her life. As a student at Oxford University, she majored in chemistry, a field dominated by men, and she became the first woman president of the Oxford University Conservative Association. A few years later, she qualified as a lawyer and practiced as a tax specialist.

In 1959, Thatcher entered politics, another overwhelmingly

male profession, when she was elected a member of Parliament. Analytical, articulate, and calm under fire, she was frequently asked by her party to face opponents in debate. Her skill and conviction may have been fired by an attitude she learned from her father, who told her, "You don't follow the crowd; you make up your own mind."

Her strong resolve and high competence earned her several government posts. It was during her tenure as secretary of state for education and science that she was referred to as "the most unpopular woman in Britain." But Thatcher didn't waver under the criticism. She continued working hard and gaining people's respect. Her reward was being named the first female prime minister in the history of Britain.

In that position, she continued to face criticism. She weathered abuse for privatizing state-owned industries, reducing the role of organized labor, sending troops to the Falkland Islands, and maintaining conservative policies against the Soviet Union. But no matter how severely she was criticized, she remained secure in her convictions and maintained her self-respect. She once said, "To me consensus seems to be the process of abandoning all beliefs, principles, values, and policies in search of something in which no one believes . . . What great cause would have been fought and won under the banner, 'I stand for consensus'?"

Thatcher stood for conviction in leadership. And as a result, the "Iron Lady," as she was called, was elected to three consecutive terms as prime minister. She is the only British leader of the modern era to achieve that.

F L E S H I N G   I T   O U T

Margaret Thatcher appeared to have no doubts about herself or her beliefs—and she was absolutely secure in her leadership as a result. That is the case for all great leaders. No one can live on a level inconsistent with the way he sees himself. You may have observed that in people. If someone sees himself as a loser, he finds a way to lose. Anytime his success surpasses his security, the result is self-destruction. That's not only true for followers, but it's also true for leaders.

Insecure leaders are dangerous—to themselves, their followers, and the organizations they lead—because a leadership position amplifies personal flaws. Whatever negative baggage you have in life only gets more difficult to bear when you're trying to lead others.

Insecure leaders have several common traits:

1. They Don't Provide Security for Others

An old saying states, "You cannot give what you do not have." Just as people without skill cannot impart skill to others, people without security cannot make others feel secure. And for a person to become an effective leader, the kind that others *want* to follow, he needs to make his followers feel good about themselves.

2. They Take More from People than They Give

Insecure people are on a continual quest for validation, acknowledgment, and love. Because of that, their focus is on finding security, not instilling it in others. They are primarily takers rather than givers, and takers do not make good leaders.

3. They Continually Limit Their Best People

Show me an insecure leader, and I'll show you someone who cannot genuinely celebrate his people's victories. He might even prevent them from realizing any victories. Or he might take credit personally for the best work of his team. As I mention in *The 21 Irrefutable Laws of Leadership*, only secure leaders give power to others. That's the Law of Empowerment. But an insecure leader hoards power. In fact, the better his people are, the more threatened he feels—and the harder he will work to limit their success and recognition.

4. They Continually Limit the Organization

When followers are undermined and receive no recognition, they become discouraged and eventually stop performing at their potential. And when that happens, the entire organization suffers.

In contrast, secure leaders are able to believe in others because they believe in themselves. They aren't arrogant; they know their own strengths and weaknesses and respect themselves. When their people perform well, they don't feel threatened. They go out of their way to bring the best people together and then build them up so that they will perform at the highest level. And when a secure leader's team succeeds, it brings him great joy. He sees that as the highest compliment he can receive for his leadership ability.

R E F L E C T I N G   O N   I T

How well do you understand and respect yourself? Do you know your strengths and feel good about them? Have you recognized your weaknesses and accepted the ones you can't change? When a person realizes that he is created with a particular personality type and has unique gifts, he is better able to appreciate the strengths and successes of others.

How secure are you as a leader? When a follower has a great idea, do you support it or suppress it? Do you celebrate your people's victories? When your team succeeds, do you give the members credit? If not, you may be dealing with insecurity, and it could be limiting you, your team, and your organization.

B R I N G I N G   I T   H O M E

To improve your security, do the following:

- *Know yourself.* If you are the kind of person who is not naturally self-aware, take time to learn about yourself. Take a personality test, such as the ones created by Myers-Briggs or Florence Littauer. Ask several people who know you well to name your three greatest talents and your three greatest weaknesses. Don't defend yourself when you hear their answers; gather the information and then reflect on it.

- *Give away the credit.* You may not believe that you can succeed if others receive the praise for the job your team is doing. Try it. If you assist others and acknowledge their contributions, you will help their careers, lift their morale, and improve the organization. And it will make you look like an effective leader.

* *Get some help*. If you cannot overcome feelings of insecurity on your own, seek professional help. Get to the root of your problems with the assistance of a good counselor, not only for your own benefit but also for that of your people.

DAILY TAKE-AWAY

French novelist Honoré de Balzac was a keen observer of human nature, and he sought to capture a complete picture of modern civilization in his huge work *The Human Comedy*. He once observed, "Nothing is a greater impediment to being on good terms with others than being ill at ease with yourself." Don't let insecurity prevent you from reaching your potential.

SELF-DISCIPLINE:

THE FIRST PERSON YOU LEAD IS YOU

The first and best victory is to conquer self.

—*Plato, Philosopher*

A man without decision of character

can never be said to belong to himself . . .

He belongs to whatever can make captive of him.

—*John Foster, Author*

KING OF THE HILL

It's a tough road to the top. Not many people ever reach the place where they are considered one of the best at their work. And even fewer are believed to be *the* best—ever. Yet that's what Jerry Rice has achieved. He is called the best person ever to play wide receiver in football. And he has got the records to prove it.

People who know him well say he is a natural. Physically his God-given gifts are incredible. He has everything a coach would want in a receiver. Hall of Fame football coach Bill Walsh said, "I don't think there's been a guy equal to him physically." Yet that alone has not made him great. The real key to his success has been his self-discipline. He works and prepares—day in and day out—unlike anyone else in professional football.

The story of Rice's ability to push himself can be told in his experiences conquering hills. The first came in high school. At the end of each practice, B. L. Moor High School Coach Charles Davis used to have his players sprint twenty times up and down a forty-yard hill. On a particularly hot and muggy Mississippi day, Rice was ready to give up after eleven trips. As he sneaked toward the locker room, he realized what he was doing. "Don't quit," he told himself. "Because once you get into that mode of quitting, then you feel like it's okay." He went back and finished his sprints, and he has never been a quitter since.

As a professional player, he has become famous for his ability to sprint up another hill. This one is a rugged 2.5-mile park trail in San Carlos, California, that Rice makes a regular part of his workout schedule. Other top players try to keep up with him on it, but they fall behind, astounded by his stamina. But that's only a part of Rice's regular routine. Even in the off-season, while other players are fishing or lying around enjoying downtime, Rice is working, his normal exercise routine lasting from 7:00 A.M. to noon. Someone once joked, "He is so well-conditioned that he makes Jamie Lee Curtis look like James Earl Jones."

"What a lot of guys don't understand about Jerry is that with him, football's a twelve-month thing," says NFL cornerback Kevin Smith. "He's a natural, but he still works. That's what separates the good from the great."

Rice recently climbed another hill in his career: he made a comeback from a devastating injury. Prior to that, he had never missed a game in nineteen seasons of football, a testament to his disciplined work ethic and absolute tenacity. When he blew out his knee on August 31, 1997, people thought he was finished for the season. After all, only one player had ever had a similar injury and come back in the same season—Rod Woodson. He had rehabilitated his knee in four and a half months. Rice did it in three and a half—through sheer grit, determination, and incredible self-discipline. People had never seen anything like it before, and they might not again. And Rice continues to build his records and his reputation while helping his team win.

FLESHING IT OUT

Jerry Rice is a perfect example of the power of self-discipline. No one achieves and sustains success without it. And no matter how gifted a leader is, his gifts will never reach their maximum potential without the application of self-discipline. It positions a leader to go to the highest level and is a key to leadership that lasts.

If you want to become a leader for whom self-discipline is an asset, follow these action points:

1. Develop and Follow Your Priorities

Anyone who does what he must only when he is in the mood or when it's convenient isn't going to be successful. Nor will people respect and follow him. Someone once said, "To do important tasks, two things are necessary: a plan and not quite enough time." As a leader, you already have too little time. Now all you need is a plan. If you can determine what's really a priority and release yourself from everything else, it's a lot easier to follow through on what's important. And that's the essence of self-discipline.

2. Make a Disciplined Lifestyle Your Goal

Learning about any highly disciplined person, such as Jerry Rice, should make you realize that to be successful, self-discipline can't be a one-time event. It has to become a lifestyle.

One of the best ways to do that is to develop systems and routines, especially in areas crucial to your long-term growth and success. For example, because I continually write and speak, I read and file material for future use every day. And since my heart attack in December 1998, I exercise every morning. It's not something I'll do just for a season. I'll do it every day for the rest of my life.

3. Challenge Your Excuses

To develop a lifestyle of discipline, one of your first tasks must be to challenge and eliminate any tendency to make excuses. As French classical writer François La Rochefoucauld said, "Almost all our faults are more pardonable than the methods we think up to hide them." If you have several reasons why you can't be self-disciplined, realize that they are really just a bunch of excuses— all of which need to be challenged if you want to go to the next level as a leader.

4. Remove Rewards Until the Job Is Done

Author Mike Delaney wisely remarked, "Any business or industry that pays equal rewards to its goof-offs and its eager-beavers sooner or later will find itself with more goof-offs than eager-beavers." If you lack self-discipline, you may be in the habit of having dessert before eating your vegetables.

A story illustrates the power of withholding rewards. An older couple had been at a campground for a couple of days when a family arrived at the site next to them. As soon as their sport-utility vehicle came to a stop, the couple and their three kids piled out. One child hurriedly unloaded ice chests, backpacks, and other items while the other two quickly put up tents. The site was ready in fifteen minutes.

The older couple was amazed. "You folks sure do work great together," the elderly gentleman told the dad admiringly.

"You just need a system," replied the dad. "Nobody goes to the bathroom until camp's set up."

5. Stay Focused on Results

Anytime you concentrate on the difficulty of the work instead of its results or rewards, you're likely to become discouraged. Dwell on it too long, and you'll develop self-pity instead of self-discipline. The next time you're facing a must-do task and you're thinking of doing what's convenient instead of paying the price, change your focus. Count the benefits of doing what's right, and then dive in.

REFLECTING ON IT

Author H. Jackson Brown Jr. quipped, "Talent without discipline is like an octopus on roller skates. There's plenty of movement, but you never know if it's going to be forward, backwards, or sideways." If you know you have talent, and you've seen a lot of motion—but little concrete results—you may lack self-discipline.

Look at last week's schedule. How much of your time did you devote to regular, disciplined activities? Did you do anything to grow and improve yourself professionally? Did you engage in activities promoting good health? Did you dedicate part of your income to savings or investments? If you've been putting off those things, telling yourself that you'll do them later, you may need to work on your self-discipline.

B R I N G I N G   I T   H O M E

To improve your self-discipline, do the following:

- *Sort out your priorities.* Think about which two or three areas of life are most important to you. Write them down, along with the disciplines that you must develop to keep growing and improving in those areas. Develop a plan to make the disciplines a daily or weekly part of your life.

- *List the reasons.* Take the time to write out the benefits of practicing the disciplines you've just listed. Then post the benefits someplace where you will see them daily. On the days when you don't want to follow through, reread your list.

- *Get rid of excuses.* Write down every reason why you might not be able to follow through with your disciplines. Read through them. You need to dismiss them as the excuses they are. Even if a reason seems legitimate, find a solution to overcome it. Don't leave yourself any reasons to quit. Remember, only in the moment of discipline do you have the power to achieve your dreams.

DAILY TAKE-AWAY

A nursery in Canada displays this sign on its wall: "The best time to plant a tree is twenty-five years ago . . . The second best time is today." Plant the tree of self-discipline in your life today.

19

SERVANTHOOD:

TO GET AHEAD, PUT OTHERS FIRST

The true leader serves. Serves people.
Serves their best interests, and in so doing
will not always be popular, may not always impress.
But because true leaders are motivated by loving
concern rather than a desire for personal glory,
they are willing to pay the price.

—*Eugene B. Habecker, Author*

You've got to love your people
more than your position.

—*John C. Maxwell*

ON SHAKY GROUND

Not long ago Americans became acquainted with U.S. Army General H. Norman Schwarzkopf. He displayed highly successful leadership abilities in commanding the allied troops in the Persian Gulf War, just as he had done throughout his career, beginning in his days at West Point.

In *The 21 Irrefutable Laws of Leadership,* I wrote how in Vietnam he turned around a battalion that was in shambles. The First Battalion of the Sixth Infantry—known as the "worst of the sixth"—went from laughingstock to effective fighting force and were selected to perform a more difficult mission. That turned out to be an assignment to what Schwarzkopf described as "a horrible, malignant place" called the Batangan Peninsula. The area had been fought over for thirty years, was covered with mines and booby traps, and was the site of numerous weekly casualties from those devices.

Schwarzkopf made the best of a bad situation. He introduced procedures to greatly reduce casualties, and whenever a soldier *was* injured by a mine, he flew out to check on the man, had him evacuated using his chopper, and talked to the other men to boost their morale.

On May 28, 1970, a man was injured by a mine, and Schwarzkopf flew to the man's location. While the helicopter was evacuating the injured soldier, another soldier stepped on a mine, severely injuring his leg. The man thrashed around on the ground, screaming and wailing. That's when everyone realized the first mine hadn't been a lone booby trap. They were all standing in the middle of a minefield.

Schwarzkopf believed the injured man could survive and even keep his leg—but only if he stopped flailing around. There was only one thing he could do. He had to go after the man and immobilize him. Schwarzkopf wrote,

> I started through the minefield, one slow step at a time, staring at the ground, looking for telltale bumps or little prongs sticking up from the dirt. My knees were shaking so hard that each time I took a step, I had to grab my leg and steady it with both hands before I could take another . . . It seemed like a thousand years before I reached the kid.

The 240-pound Schwarzkopf, who had been a wrestler at West Point, then pinned the wounded man and calmed him down. It saved his life. And with the help of an engineer team, Schwarzkopf got him and the others out of the minefield.

The quality that Schwarzkopf displayed that day could be described as heroism, courage, or even foolhardiness. But I think the word that best describes it is *servanthood*. On that day in May, the only way he could be effective as a leader was to serve the soldier who was in trouble.

FLESHING IT OUT

When you think of servanthood, do you envision it as an activity performed by relatively low-skilled people at the bottom of the positional totem pole? If you do, you have a wrong impression. Servanthood is not about position or skill. It's about attitude. You have undoubtedly met people in service positions who have poor attitudes toward servanthood: the rude worker at the government agency, the waiter who can't be bothered with taking your order, the store clerk who talks on the phone with a friend instead of helping you.

Just as you can sense when a worker doesn't want to help people, you can just as easily detect whether a leader has a servant's heart. And the truth is that the best leaders desire to serve others, not themselves.

What does it mean to embody the quality of servanthood? A true servant leader:

1. Puts Others Ahead of His Own Agenda
The first mark of servanthood is the ability to put others ahead of yourself and your personal desires. It is more than being willing to put your agenda on hold. It means intentionally being aware of your people's needs, available to help them, and able to accept their desires as important.

2. Possesses the Confidence to Serve
The real heart of servanthood is security. Show me someone who thinks he is too important to serve, and I'll show you someone who is basically insecure. How we treat others is really a reflection of how we think about ourselves. Philosopher-poet Eric Hoffer captured that thought:

The remarkable thing is that we really love our neighbor as ourselves; we do unto others as we do unto ourselves. We hate others when we hate ourselves. We are tolerant toward others when we tolerate ourselves. We forgive others when we forgive ourselves. It is not love of self but hatred of self which is at the root of the troubles that afflict our world.

The Law of Empowerment says that only secure leaders give power to others. It's also true that only secure leaders exhibit servanthood.

3. Initiates Service to Others
Just about anyone will serve if compelled to do so. And some will serve in a crisis. But you can really see the heart of someone who initiates service to others. Great leaders see the need, seize the opportunity, and serve without expecting anything in return.

4. Is Not Position-Conscious
Servant leaders don't focus on rank or position. When Colonel Norman Schwarzkopf stepped into that minefield, rank was the last thing on his mind. He was one person trying to help another. If anything, being the leader gave him a greater sense of obligation to serve.

5. Serves Out of Love
Servanthood is not motivated by manipulation or self-promotion.

It is fueled by love. In the end, the extent of your influence depends on the depth of your concern for others. That's why it's so important for leaders to be willing to serve.

REFLECTING ON IT

Where is your heart when it comes to serving others? Do you desire to become a leader for the perks and benefits? Or are you motivated by a desire to help others?

If you really want to become the kind of leader that people want to follow, you will have to settle the issue of servanthood. If your attitude is to be served rather than to serve, you may be headed for trouble. If this is an issue in your life, then heed this advice:

Stop lording over people, and *start* listening to them.
Stop role-playing for advancement, and *start* risking for others' benefit.
Stop seeking your own way, and *start* serving others.

It is true that those who would be great must be like the least and the servant of all.

BRINGING IT HOME

To improve your servanthood, do the following:

- *Perform small acts.* When was the last time you performed small acts of kindness for others? Start with those closest to you: your spouse, children, parents. Find ways today to do small things that show others you care.

- *Learn to walk slowly through the crowd.* One of the greatest lessons I learned as a young leader came from my father. I call it walking slowly through the crowd. The next time you attend a function with a number of clients, colleagues, or employees, make it your goal to connect with others by circulating among them and talking to people. Focus on each person you meet. Learn his name if you don't know it already. Make your agenda getting to know each person's needs, wants, and desires. Then later when you go home, make a note to yourself to do something beneficial for half a dozen of those people.

- *Move into action.* If an attitude of servanthood is conspicuously absent from your life, the best way to change it is to start serving. Begin serving with your body, and your heart will eventually catch up. Sign up to serve others for six months at your church, a community agency, or a volunteer organization. If your attitude still isn't good at the end of your term, do it again. Keep at it until your heart changes.

DAILY TAKE-AWAY

Albert Schweitzer wisely stated, "I don't know what your destiny will be, but one thing I know: The ones among you who will be really happy are those who have sought and found how to serve." If you want to lead on the highest level, be willing to serve on the lowest.

20

TEACHABILITY:

TO KEEP LEADING, KEEP LEARNING

Value your listening and reading time at
roughly ten times your talking time. This will assure
you that you are on a course of continuous
learning and self-improvement.

—Gerald McGinnis,
President and CEO of Respironics, Inc.

It's what you learn after you know it all that counts.

—John Wooden, Hall of Fame Basketball Coach

SUCCESS DISGUISED AS A TRAMP

If you see the image of a little man sporting a tiny moustache, carrying a cane, and wearing baggy pants, big, clumsy shoes, and a derby hat, you know immediately that it's Charlie Chaplin. Just about everyone recognizes him. In the 1910s and 1920s, he was *the* most famous and recognizable person on the planet. If we looked at today's celebrities, the only person even in the same category as Chaplin in popularity would be Michael Jordan. And to measure who is the bigger star, we would have to wait another seventy-five years to find out how well everyone remembers Michael.

When Chaplin was born, nobody would have predicted great fame for him. Born into poverty as the son of English music hall performers, he found himself on the street as a small child when his mother was institutionalized. After years in workhouses and orphanages, he began working on the stage to support himself. By age seventeen, he was a veteran performer. In 1914, while in his mid-twenties, he worked for Mack Sennett at Keystone Studios in Hollywood making $150 a week. During that first year in the movie business, he made thirty-five films working as an actor, writer, and director. Everyone recognized his talent immediately, and his popularity grew. A year later, he earned $1,250 a week. Then in 1918, he did something unheard of. He signed the entertainment industry's first $1 million contract. He was rich; he was famous; and he was the most powerful filmmaker in the world—at the ripe old age of twenty-nine.

Chaplin was successful because he had great talent and incredible drive. But those traits were fueled by teachability. He continually strived to grow, learn, and perfect his craft. Even when he was the most popular and highest paid performer *in the world,* he wasn't content with the status quo.

Chaplin explained his desire to improve to an interviewer:

> When I am watching one of my pictures presented to an audience, I always pay close attention to what they don't laugh at. If, for example, several audiences do not laugh at a stunt I mean to be funny, I at once begin to tear that trick to pieces and try to discover what was wrong in the idea or in the execution of it. If I hear a slight ripple at something I had not expected to be funny, I ask myself why that particular thing got a laugh.

That desire to grow made him successful economically, and it brought a high level of excellence to everything he did. In those early days, Chaplin's work was hailed as marvelous entertainment. As time went by, he was recognized as a comic genius. Today many of his movies are considered masterpieces, and he is appreciated as one of the greatest filmmakers of all time. Screenwriter and film critic James Agee wrote, "The finest pantomime, the deepest emotion, the richest and most poignant poetry were in Chaplin's work."

If Chaplin had replaced his teachability with arrogant self-satisfaction when he became successful, his name would be right up there along with Ford Sterling or Ben Turpin, stars of silent films who are all but forgotten today. But Chaplin kept growing and learning as an actor, director, and eventually film executive. When he learned from experience that filmmakers were at the mercy of studios and distributors, he started his own organization, United Artists, along with Douglas Fairbanks, Mary Pickford, and D. W. Griffith. The film company is still in business today.

FLESHING IT OUT

Leaders face the danger of contentment with the *status quo*. After all, if a leader already possesses influence and has achieved a level of respect, why should he keep growing? The answer is simple:

> Your growth determines who you are.
>
> Who you are determines who you attract.
>
> Who you attract determines the success of your organization.

If you want to grow your organization, *you* have to remain teachable.

Allow me to give you five guidelines to help you cultivate and maintain a teachable attitude:

1. Cure Your Destination Disease
Ironically, lack of teachability is often rooted in achievement. Some people mistakenly believe that if they can accomplish a particular goal, they no longer have to grow. It can happen with almost anything: earning a degree, reaching a desired position, receiving a particular award, or achieving a financial goal.

But effective leaders cannot afford to think that way. The day they stop growing is the day they forfeit their potential—and the potential of the organization. Remember the words of Ray Kroc: "As long as you're green, you're growing. As soon as you're ripe, you start to rot."

2. Overcome Your Success
Another irony of teachability is that success often hinders it. Effective leaders know that what got them there doesn't keep them there. If you have been successful in the past, beware. And consider this: if what you did yesterday still looks big to you, you haven't done much today.

3. Swear Off Shortcuts
My friend Nancy Dornan says, "The longest distance between two points is a shortcut." That's really true. For everything of value in life, you pay a price. As you desire to grow in a particular area, figure out what it will really take, including the price, and then determine to pay it.

4. Trade In Your Pride
Teachability requires us to admit we don't know everything, and that can make us look bad. In addition, if we keep learning, we must also keep making mistakes. But as writer and expert craftsman Elbert Hubbard said, "The greatest mistake one can make in life is to be continually fearing you will make one." You cannot be prideful and teachable at the same time.

Emerson wrote, "For everything you gain, you lose something." To gain growth, give up your pride.

5. Never Pay Twice for the Same Mistake

Teddy Roosevelt asserted, "He who makes no mistakes, makes no progress." That's true. But the leader who keeps making *the same* mistakes also makes no progress. As a teachable leader, you will make mistakes. Forget them, but always remember what they taught you. If you don't, you will pay for them more than once.

REFLECTING ON IT

When I was a kid growing up in rural Ohio, I saw this sign in a feed store: "If you don't like the crop you are reaping, check the seed you are sowing." Though the sign was an ad for seeds, it contained a wonderful principle.

What kind of crop are you reaping? Do your life and leadership seem to be getting better day after day, month after month, year after year? Or are you constantly fighting just to hold your ground? If you're not where you hoped you would be by this time in your life, your problem may be lack of teachability. When was the last time you did something for the first time? When was the last time you made yourself vulnerable by diving into something for which you weren't the expert? Observe your attitude toward growing and learning during the next several days or weeks to see where you stand.

BRINGING IT HOME

To improve your teachability, do the following:

- *Observe how you react to mistakes.* Do you admit your mistakes? Do you apologize when appropriate? Or are you defensive? Observe yourself. And ask a trusted friend's opinion. If you react badly—or you make no mistakes at all— you need to work on your teachability.

- *Try something new.* Go out of your way today to do something different that will stretch you mentally, emotionally, or physically. Challenges change us for the better. If you really want to start growing, make new challenges part of your daily activities.

- *Learn in your area of strength.* Read six to twelve books a year on leadership or your field of specialization. Continuing to learn in an area where you are already an expert prevents you from becoming jaded and unteachable.

DAILY TAKE-AWAY

After winning his third world championship, bull rider Tuff Hedeman didn't have a big celebration. He moved on to Denver to start the new season—and the whole process over again. His comment: "The bull won't care what I did last week." Whether you're an untested rookie or a successful veteran, if you want to be a champion tomorrow, be teachable today.

VISION:
YOU CAN SEIZE ONLY
WHAT YOU CAN SEE

A great leader's courage to fulfill his vision
comes from passion, not position.

—John C. Maxwell

.

The future belongs to those who see possibilities
before they become obvious.

—John Sculley
Former CEO of Pepsi and Apple Computer

No Chipped Paint . . .
All the Horses Jump

One of the great dreamers of the twentieth century was Walt Disney. Any person who could create the first sound cartoon, first all-color cartoon, and first animated feature-length motion picture is definitely someone with vision. But Disney's greatest masterpieces of vision were Disneyland and Walt Disney World. And the spark for that vision came from an unexpected place.

Back when Walt's two daughters were young, he used to take them to an amusement park in the Los Angeles area on Saturday mornings. His girls loved it, and he did too. An amusement park is a kid's paradise, with wonderful atmosphere: the smell of popcorn and cotton candy, the gaudy colors of signs advertising rides, and the sound of kids screaming as the roller coaster plummets over a hill.

Walt was especially captivated by the carousel. As he approached it, he saw a blur of bright images racing around to the tune of energetic calliope music. But when he got closer and the carousel stopped, he could see that his eye had been fooled. He observed shabby horses with cracked and chipped paint. And he noticed that only the horses on the outside row moved up and down. The others stood lifeless, bolted to the floor.

The cartoonist's disappointment inspired him with a grand vision. In his mind's eye he could see an amusement park where the illusion didn't evaporate, where children and adults could enjoy a carnival atmosphere without the seedy side that accompanies some circuses or traveling carnivals. His dream became Disneyland. As Larry Taylor stated in *Be an Orange,* Walt's vision could be summarized as, "No chipped paint. All the horses jump."

Vision is everything for a leader. It is utterly indispensable. Why? Because vision leads the leader. It paints the target. It sparks and fuels the fire within, and draws him forward. It is also the fire lighter for others who follow that leader. Show me a leader without vision, and I'll show you someone who isn't going anywhere. At best, he is traveling in circles.

To get a handle on vision and how it comes to be a part of a good leader's life, understand these things:

1. Vision Starts Within

When I'm teaching at conferences, someone will occasionally ask me to give him a vision for his organization. But I can't do it. You can't buy, beg, or borrow vision. It has to come from the inside. For Disney, vision was never a problem. Because of his creativity and desire for excellence, he always saw what *could* be.

If you lack vision, look inside yourself. Draw on your natural gifts and desires. Look to your calling if you have one. And if you still don't sense a vision of your own, then consider hooking up with a leader whose vision resonates with you. Become his partner. That's what Walt Disney's brother, Roy, did. He was a good businessman and leader who could make things happen, but Walt was the one who provided the vision. Together, they made an incredible team.

2. Vision Draws on Your History
Vision isn't some mystical quality that comes out of a vacuum, as some people seem to believe. It grows from a leader's past and the history of the people around him. That was the case for Disney. But it's true for all leaders. Talk to any leader, and you're likely to discover key events in his past that were instrumental in the creation of his vision.

3. Vision Meets Others' Needs
True vision is far-reaching. It goes beyond what one individual can accomplish. And if it has real value, it does more than just *include* others; it *adds value* to them. If you have a vision that doesn't serve others, it's probably too small.

4. Vision Helps You Gather Resources
One of the most valuable benefits of vision is that it acts like a magnet—attracting, challenging, and uniting people. It also rallies finances and other resources. The greater the vision, the more winners it has the potential to attract. The more challenging the vision, the harder the participants fight to achieve it. Edwin Land, the founder of Polaroid, advised, "The first thing you do is teach

the person to feel that the vision is very important and nearly impossible. That draws out the drive in winners."

Where does vision come from? To find the vision that is indispensable to leadership, you have to become a good listener. You must listen to several voices.

The Inner Voice

As I have already said, vision starts within. Do you know your life's mission? What stirs your heart? What do you dream about? If what you're pursuing in life doesn't come from a desire within—from the very depths of who you are and what you believe—you will not be able to accomplish it.

The Unhappy Voice

Where does inspiration for great ideas come from? From noticing what *doesn't* work. Discontent with the *status quo* is a great catalyst for vision. Are you on complacent cruise control? Or do you find yourself itching to change your world? No great leader in history has fought to prevent change.

The Successful Voice

Nobody can accomplish great things alone. To fulfill a big vision, you need a good team. But you also need good advice from someone who is ahead of you in the leadership journey. If you want to lead others to greatness, find a mentor. Do you have an adviser who can help you sharpen your vision?

The Higher Voice

Although it's true that your vision must come from within, you shouldn't let it be confined by your limited capabilities. A truly valuable vision must have God in it. Only He knows your full capabilities. Have you looked beyond yourself, even beyond your own lifetime, as you've sought your vision? If not, you may be missing your true potential and life's best for you.

B R I N G I N G   I T   H O M E

To improve your vision, do the following:

- *Measure yourself.* If you have previously thought about the vision for your life and articulated it, measure how well you are carrying it out. Talk to several key people, such as your spouse, a close friend, and key employees, asking them to state what they think your vision is. If *they* can articulate it, then *you* are probably living it.

- *Write it down.* If you've thought about your vision but never put it in writing, take the time to do it today. Writing clarifies your thinking. Once you've written it, evaluate whether it is worthy of your life's best. And then pursue it with all you've got.

- Do *a gut check*. If you haven't done a lot of work on vision, spend the next several weeks or months thinking about it. Consider what really impacts you at a gut level.

What makes you cry? _____

What makes you dream? _____

What gives you energy? _____

Also think about what you'd like to see change in the world around you. What do you see that isn't—but could be? Once your ideas start to become clearer, write them down and talk to a mentor about them.

DAILY TAKE-AWAY

From 1923 to 1955, Robert Woodruff served as president of Coca-Cola. During that time, he wanted Coca-Cola to be available to every American serviceman around the world for five cents, no matter what it cost the company. What a bold goal! But it was nothing compared to the bigger picture he could see in his mind's eye. In his lifetime, he wanted every person in the *world* to have tasted Coca-Cola. When you look deep into your heart and soul for a vision, what do *you* see?

CONCLUSION

I hope you have enjoyed reading *The 21 Indispensable Qualities of a Leader* and have benefited from doing the exercises in the "Bringing It Home" section of each chapter. These assignments are designed to help you get a handle on each quality and start you on the process of continuous personal growth in your life.

I want to encourage you to keep growing as a leader. Review this book periodically to measure how you're developing. And put yourself on a regular program where you consistently read books, listen to tapes, and attend conferences that stretch you.

I also want to encourage you to find other leaders who will mentor you in person or through books and tapes. The only way to become the kind of leader that people *want* to follow is to keep growing and learning about leadership. Good luck in your journey.

About the Author

JOHN C. MAXWELL is an internationally recognized leadership expert, speaker, and author who has sold over 13 million books. His organizations have trained more than 2 million leaders worldwide. Dr. Maxwell is the founder of EQUIP and INJOY Stewardship Services. Every year he speaks to Fortune 500 companies, international government leaders, and audiences as diverse as the United States Military Academy at West Point, the National Football League, and ambassadors at the United Nations. A *New York Times*, *Wall Street Journal*, and *Business Week* bestselling author, Maxwell was named the World's Top Leadership Guru by Leadershipgurus.net. He was also one of only 25 authors and artists named to Amazon.com's 10th Anniversary Hall of Fame. Three of his books, *The 21 Irrefutable Laws of Leadership*, *Developing the Leader Within You*, and *The 21 Indispensable Qualities of a Leader* have each sold over a million copies.

BOOKS BY DR. JOHN C. MAXWELL
CAN TEACH YOU HOW TO BE A **REAL** SUCCESS

RELATIONSHIPS

Be a People Person

Becoming a Person of Influence

Relationships 101

The Power of Influence

The Power of Partnership in the Church

The Treasure of a Friend

Ethics 101

Winning with People

25 Ways to Win with People

ATTITUDE

Be All You Can Be

Failing Forward

The Power of Thinking Big

Living at the Next Level

Think on These Things

The Winning Attitude

Your Bridge to a Better Future

The Power of Attitude

Attitude 101

Thinking for a Change

The Difference Maker

The Journey from Success to Significance

EQUIPPING

Developing the Leaders Around You

Equipping 101

The 17 Indisputable Laws of Teamwork

The 17 Essential Qualities of a Team Player

Partners in Prayer

Your Road Map for Success

Success One Day at a Time

Today Matters

Talent Is Never Enough

LEADERSHIP

The 21 Indispensable Qualities of a Leader

Revised & Updated 10th Anniversary Edition of *The 21 Irrefutable Laws of Leadership*

The 21 Most Powerful Minutes in a Leader's Day

Developing the Leader Within You

Leadership 101

Leadership Promises for Every Day

The 360 Degree Leader

The Right to Lead

The Power of Leadership

Leadership Gold

Go For Gold

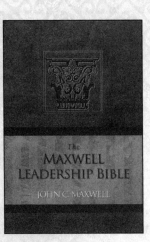

ISBN: 0-7180-1344-1

The *Maxwell Leadership Bible* shows us what God's Word has to say about leaders and leadership. Executive Editor John C. Maxwell has assembled biblical teaching to equip and encourage leaders and those who serve with them, to meet 21st-century challenges by using the time-tested and irrefutable principles of leadership that God has shown us in the Bible.

THOMAS NELSON
Since 1798

For other products and live events,
visit us at: thomasnelson.com